At David C Cook, we equip the local church around
the corner and around the globe to make disciples.
Come see how we are working together—go to
www.davidccook.org. Thank you!

DAVID C COOK

transforming lives together

What people are saying about ...

SO THE NEXT GENERATION WILL KNOW

"Though times have changed, the mandate for faithful parenting hasn't. *So the Next Generation Will Know* creates a bridge between the uncertain tides of modernity and the biblical expectations for teaching children. It provides helpful principles that equip parents and even youth pastors for reaching, instructing, and molding the hearts of the next generation."

Dr. R. Albert Mohler Jr., president of The
Southern Baptist Theological Seminary

"This may be the most important Christian book of the year! What's more vital than understanding how to teach the truth of Christianity to the next generation? Let this book coach you in equipping and encouraging the Christian leaders of tomorrow. The obstacles are great, but the opportunities are greater still!"

Lee Strobel, bestselling author of *The
Case for Christ* and *The Case for Faith*

"Sean and Jim are absolutely on target—we *must* be intentional in loving and equipping the next generation with the truth about God and the truth of God. This is no 'fluffy' book, but a challenging and exceptional book for parents, grandparents, and youth workers who all care about those we are sending to a time we will not see."

Dr. Dennis Rainey, cofounder of FamilyLife

"After thirty years practicing pediatric medicine and speaking to thousands of kids across America, I have never seen such confusion, angst, and anxiety among our kids. They need help in the form of sound and clear teaching about the biblical truths that those of us with faith can offer. Sean McDowell and J. Warner Wallace are the perfect men to do that. This will make an extraordinary impact on the next generation."

Meg Meeker, MD, author of the national bestseller *Strong Fathers, Strong Daughters*

"*So the Next Generation Will Know* is an important book for today. Parents and teachers and pastors need all the help they can get.... This new book provides great tips to help them teach their kids a Christian worldview and pave the way for their bright future!"

George Foreman, two-time world heavyweight champion, Olympic gold medalist, and pastor of The Church of the Lord Jesus Christ

"*So the Next Generation Will Know* is a clarion call for youth influencers to be intentional and strategic in how they minister to students today. Based on in-depth research and personal experience, Sean and J. Warner offer practical strategies for parents, youth workers, and teachers to equip this new generation with biblical truth. If you are looking to have lasting impact on young people today, this book will be your indispensable guide."

Doug Fields, veteran youth pastor, author of *Purpose-Driven Youth Ministry*, and cofounder of Downloadyouthministry.com

"When two preeminent apologists like Sean McDowell and J. Warner Wallace combine their intellect, heart, and soul to write a book, I immediately think, *I must have this book as a resource!* I was not disappointed. Get this book. It is such a great resource."

Dr. Derwin L. Gray, lead-elder pastor of Transformation Church and author of *High Definition Leader: Building Multiethnic Churches in a Multiethnic World*

"If you work with students and want to learn how to more effectively pass on your faith to the next generation, start *here*. Whether you are a parent, youth leader, or teacher, you will find practical, actionable ideas about how to give your students a biblical worldview. In this clearly written, creative, and well-researched book, learn from Sean McDowell and J. Warner Wallace as they share from their wealth of experience training the next generation. Start experimenting, and watch the students you work with come alive and want to take their faith seriously! This book is a game changer for your youth ministry."

Jonathan Morrow, author of *Welcome to College* and creator of *5 Things Every Teenager Needs to Build a Lasting Faith*

"*So the Next Generation Will Know* is a must read for every Christian believer. This book helps both parents and teachers connect with youth and answers pertinent questions that arise about Christianity."

Brett Hundley, NFL quarterback
with the Seattle Seahawks

"The time when young people are most likely to abandon their Christian upbringing is in their teens. And the reason most often given is unanswered doubts and questions. It's time for parents, pastors, teachers, and youth leaders to step to the plate and provide answers to those questions. Sean McDowell and J. Warner Wallace have spent years working with teens, and it shows. This book is clear, readable, and practical. It will provide you with motivation and creative tips on how to structure teaching on worldview and apologetics into your family, church, or school."

Nancy Pearcey, author of *Total Truth*
and *Love Thy Body: Answering Hard
Questions about Life and Sexuality*

"*So the Next Generation Will Know* is an impassioned call to purposefully pour into our young people and love, train, and unleash them with the message and mission of Jesus. As founder and CEO of Dare 2 Share, mobilizing teenagers to know and share their faith is near and dear to my heart. But this book's message also resonates with me on a personal level. Raised in a violent, crime-ridden, inner-city family, I was deeply impacted as a teenager by the kind of theologically robust, activation-oriented youth group McDowell and Wallace champion within these pages. This practical primer is packed with field-tested ideas that help adults raise the bar for teenagers and nudge them beyond their comfort zone so they'll grow deeper in their walk with Jesus as they go wider into the world with His message."

Greg Stier, founder and CEO of Dare 2 Share Ministries

"My go-to resource from two guys who not only 'get' Gen Z, but also know how to reach them!"

Jonathan McKee, author of *The Teen's Guide to Social Media and Mobile Devices*

"*So the Next Generation Will Know* equips parents, educators, pastors, and all of us to be more effective at engaging Gen Z to love God and others. We all have a responsibility to help our kids and the next generation find its way back to God, and this book by J. Warner Wallace and Sean McDowell will be a big help!"

Dave Ferguson, lead pastor at Community Christian Church and author of *Finding Your Way Back to God*

"As someone who has given my life's work to engaging teenagers with the love of Jesus, I wish every person in every pew would read this book and engage our collective responsibility to the amazing young people in our midst. The honest truth is that I wasn't sure I would resonate with this book, because, while I have deep respect for the authors, I am also aware that we have somewhat differing worldviews and theological constructs. But I absolutely loved it—personal and practical and focused on the right things."

Mark Oestreicher, partner at the Youth
Cartel and author of more than sixty
books, including *Youth Ministry 3.0*

"Sean and J. Warner show us how to develop a deeper relationship with our teens in a digital age and how to walk beside them in their curiosity for the Truth! As parents of three boys entering their teen years, we received help from this book to obtain the tools to keep a deeper relationship—through God—with our children. I recommend it for anyone with young people in their lives asking the tough questions."

Melissa Joan Hart, actress and star of
*God's Not Dead 2, Clarissa Explains It All,
Melissa and Joey,* and *No Good Nick*

"As a mom to six young men, I believe the practical wisdom gleaned through McDowell and Wallace's compelling research and its implications couldn't be timelier and more needed in the church. For parents, teachers, leaders, content creators, ministers, and all those who desire to see future Christ followers walk with clarity and conviction, *So the Next Generation Will Know* is a must read."

Ruth Chou Simons, artist, speaker, author
of the bestselling book *GraceLaced*,
and founder of GraceLaced.com

Sean McDowell
and
J. Warner Wallace

SO THE
NEXT
GENERATION
WILL
KNOW

*Preparing Young Christians
for a Challenging World*

DAVID C COOK™

transforming lives together

SO THE NEXT GENERATION WILL KNOW
Published by David C Cook
4050 Lee Vance Drive
Colorado Springs, CO 80918 U.S.A.

Integrity Music Limited, a Division of David C Cook
Brighton, East Sussex BN1 2RE, England

The graphic circle C logo is a registered trademark of David C Cook.

The website addresses recommended throughout this book are offered as a
resource to you. These websites are not intended in any way to be or imply an
endorsement on the part of David C Cook, nor do we vouch for their content.

Details in some stories have been changed to protect
the identities of the persons involved.

Unless otherwise noted, all Scripture quotations are taken from the ESV®
Bible (The Holy Bible, English Standard Version®), copyright © 2001 by
Crossway, a publishing ministry of Good News Publishers. Used by permission.
All rights reserved. Scripture quotations marked NASB are taken from the
New American Standard Bible®, copyright © 1960, 1995 by The Lockman
Foundation. Used by permission. (www.Lockman.org); and NIV are taken
from THE HOLY BIBLE, NEW INTERNATIONAL VERSION®, NIV® Copyright ©
1973, 2011 by Biblica, Inc.® Used by permission. All rights reserved worldwide.
The authors have added italics to Scripture quotations for emphasis.

LCCN 2019930151
ISBN 978-1-4347-1228-8
eISBN 978-0-8307-7714-3

© 2019 James Warner Wallace and Sean McDowell
Published in association with the literary agency of Mark
Sweeney & Associates, Naples, FL 34113.

The Team: Stephanie Bennett, Amy Konyndyk, Jack Campbell, Susan Murdock
Cover Design: Nick Lee

Printed in the United States of America
First Edition 2019

1 2 3 4 5 6 7 8 9 10

022819

THE AUTHORS

Sean McDowell, PhD, is an associate professor of Christian apologetics at Talbot School of Theology, Biola University, as well as a part-time high school teacher at Capistrano Valley Christian Schools. He is a bestselling author (or coauthor) of more than eighteen books, including *A New Kind of Apologist*.

Sean is a popular speaker at camps, conferences, universities, and churches worldwide. He is also the National Spokesman for Summit Ministries, a worldview training ministry for students sixteen to twenty-five. Sean lives in Southern California with his wife and three kids. You can learn more about Sean McDowell's ministry at SeanMcDowell.org.

J. Warner Wallace is a *Dateline*-featured cold-case detective, Senior Fellow at the Colson Center for Christian Worldview, adjunct professor of Christian apologetics at Talbot School of Theology, Biola University, and faculty member at Summit Worldview Conference. He is the author of *Cold-Case Christianity*, *God's Crime Scene*, and *Forensic Faith*, and is the creator (along with his wife, Susie) of the Case Makers Academy for Kids (CaseMakersAcademy.com).

J. Warner served as a children's minister, youth pastor, and lead pastor before becoming a popular national speaker. He and Susie live in Southern California and have four grown children. You can learn more about J. Warner's ministry at ColdCaseChristianity.com.

Sean: This book is dedicated to the significant adults who personally shaped me as a young man so that I could come to know the Christian faith and pass it on to the next generation.

Jim: This book is dedicated to Don Overstreet, my seminary thesis adviser and dear friend. I miss you, Don, but I hope this book reflects your Christlike character and your love for young believers.

CONTENTS

SECTION 2

FOREWORD

I grew up in a household where we went to church most Sundays. I checked all the boxes of what I thought a Christian should be. I believed in God, a power greater than myself. I had a faith, but no foundation for my faith. It was more of an influence from my mom and was just familiar to me. It wasn't until my first year of college at Michigan State that I had an experience that changed everything for me. My faith became personal to me and my relationship with Christ continues to transform me today.

In 2007, I moved up north to East Lansing, Michigan. I had just had my throwing shoulder surgically repaired, which was a relief, but a long road to recovery lay ahead. In addition to a completely new life and mental adjustment, I had several other things going on that were difficult to handle. One day in a parking garage, alone and confused, I realized I could not do any of it on my own. I began to cry, and in that moment, something amazing happened. I prayed to God, "I don't know what is happening or why, but I trust You. I don't know why I am in Michigan, but I trust You. I give everything to You, Lord. Guide me." I surrendered my life to Christ. My life did not take a magical turn where everything was perfect, but my entire perspective shifted, and I began to live differently.

That challenging time and moment of vulnerability gave me the strength to get where I am today. From then on, my faith moved to the forefront of every decision I made and was at the heart of how I dealt with adversity. I faced many more challenges, but like a muscle, the stronger my faith grew, the better I became at dealing with the circumstances that rocked me. Even in my greatest moments, when most people assumed my life was perfect, I shared truthfully that it was not perfect, but there was a reason for it all.

Fast-forward to February 4, 2018, when I quarterbacked for the Philadelphia Eagles in the Super Bowl. We beat the New England Patriots 41–33 to secure the Eagles' first-ever Super Bowl victory. Following the game, I hoisted the Lombardi Trophy and accepted the Super Bowl MVP honors in disbelief at what was happening. This was one of the greatest moments an athlete could experience! There was no doubt that I felt an immense sense of joy—looking at my team-mates and their families' faces and recalling the journey it took us all to get there. I felt incredibly grateful to be holding my daughter and standing with my wife onstage, knowing they were more important to me than any victory. Most would think that total fulfillment would be found in this moment. Yet, how many times do we hear how empty someone can still feel after a huge accomplishment. They often think that there must be more than what they are experiencing.

The following morning in a press conference, everyone wanted to hear what it felt like to be the Super Bowl MVP. My thoughts kind of shifted to how fulfilled I already was without the trophy or the victory. I began to think of all the challenging times that had shaped me, and my answer that resonated with many was, "If something is going on in your life where you are struggling, embrace it because you are growing." I realized right then and there that this was not about the trophy or the win, but about what the Lord had done in my life and the responsibility and platform I was about to have to share His love with others. My moment of true fulfillment was born in East Lansing ten years earlier. That was the moment I was truly fulfilled with the love of Christ and the solid foundation on which I could move forward.

Standing at the podium, there was so much I wanted to convey to everyone who was watching. This victory was not my life and did not complete me. It was the brutal experiences along the way that had allowed me to be where I was and the love of Christ that had brought me to that point of victory. This is the truth we need to be sure our teens are hearing at every possible opportunity.

We live in a day and age where people put on facades, especially our teens. They want to appear perfect with everything under control, yet with all the pressures, almost everyone deals with some type of anxiety or depression at some point in his or her life. Jim and Sean do a great job sharing how to first connect with younger generations and then help them through these obstacles. My prayer is that *So the Next Generation Will Know* may impact countless people so all generations can communicate with each other effectively and go through life knowing Christ and His truth.

Nick Foles

NFL quarterback, MVP of Super Bowl LII, and
author of Believe It: My Journey of Success,
Failure, and Overcoming the Odds

LOVE *SACRIFICES*

He established a testimony in Jacob
and appointed a law in Israel,
which he commanded our fathers
to teach to their children,
that the next generation might know them,
the children yet unborn,
and arise and tell them to their children,
so that they should set their hope in God
and not forget the works of God,
but keep his commandments.

Psalm 78:5–7

As I (J. Warner) stepped lightly into the row of seats, I could feel the floor sticking to my shoes. The sound of laughter filled the theater as children hurried to find their place. My kids were also eager to take their seats in the middle of the row. I nestled in next to my daughter and prepared for yet another animated, G-rated movie. I couldn't remember the last time I'd seen anything other than a children's film. I looked across the span of our four children and caught my wife sending me a knowing smile. Oh well, here we go again.

If you've raised kids, you probably remember that season of parenting in which you *intentionally* limited your choices. What movies did you watch as a family? Probably not murder mysteries or romantic comedies, right? Where did you go for dinner? Not expensive French bistros, we suspect. What kind of vacations did you take? We're guessing that Disney World was more likely the destination than the romantic island resort you had in mind as a couple.

Why do we, as parents, make these kinds of choices (and indeed sacrifices) during the parenting years? Here's why: when it comes to raising our kids, we're willing to defer our desires to do what's best for our *children*, even if it's not what we want at the time. We understand our parental duty, and we willingly make our kids our priority, so the next generation will proudly (and successfully) continue the family name.

Our extended *Christian* family is no different. Young believers may not be our biological kids, but they're ours, all the same. Together, as brothers and sisters who share the same heavenly Father, we have a duty to make kids our priority, so the next generation will proudly (and successfully) continue the family name.

Prioritizing young people will require us to defer *our* desires and do what's best for them, even if it might be inconvenient for us at the time.

As authors and public speakers, we've had the distinct privilege and opportunity to teach the church about the truth of Christianity and the nature of the Christian worldview. We've done this at Christian camps, conferences, and churches, and the vast majority of our audiences are junior high and high school students. We've also *parented* teenagers, *pastored* this age group, and *taught* them in the Christian high school setting. Here's what we've learned: if you're someone who loves young Christians, either as a parent, youth worker, educator, or fellow member of the Christian family, *now is the time to refocus*.

Jesus said that there is no greater love than laying down one's life for a friend (John 15:13). Our sacrifices reveal our priorities. If we truly love the next generation, we'll do whatever it takes to make sure they know and embrace the truth. After all, isn't that what previous generations did for each of us? Whether it was a mentor, parent, youth pastor, teacher, or coach—*someone helped us come to know the Lord*. Someone sacrificed for each of us. If we care about young people, we'll *sacrifice* for them because we *love* them.

I (Sean) sat in the local coffee shop with one of my young children. The fifty-plus-year-old man sitting next to me leaned over and interrupted our conversation. As best as I can remember, he said, "Good for you for spending time with your kids. My kids are out of the house now, but when they were younger, I made them a priority." He paused as he shifted back into his chair. Then he turned toward us again and said these last words, "Ultimately, it cost me a ton of money in my business to spend time with my kids. But I don't regret it for a second. It is one of the best decisions I ever made. After all, what's more important than investing in the next generation?" I was encouraged but also mildly convicted—was I really as committed to the next generation as this man assumed I was?

The reality is, we don't parent our kids for long, and we only get one chance to guide them through their elementary, junior high, and high school years. This season passes quickly, and it requires inten-tionality. While true for our biological children, it's also true for the young people in our church family. The next generation of Christians faces spiritual, emotional, intellectual, and moral challenges like no prior group of believers. And much of this is because of the ubiquity of technology. Members of Generation Z face more challenges just one click away than previous generations did when they would look for it.

That's why we wrote this book.

We've written many books that make the case for God and Christianity. Those books describe *what* is true and *why* we should believe it.

This book is *different*.

We wrote it for a very practical reason: to show you *how* to teach the truth of Christianity to the next generation, given the special challenges they face and their unique identity. In essence, this is not a "what is true" book; it's a "how to explain what is true" book. We've tried to write it with four groups in mind: parents, youth workers, Christian educators, and people who love young people and recognize the challenges they are facing. You probably fit into one of these four categories, and this book will give you practical advice for effectively communicating truth to this new generation of young people.

Time is short, the challenges are pressing, and the need is great. Now, more than ever, we must embrace strategies that will help young people set their hope in God, remember the works of God, and keep the commands of God—*so that the next generation will know*.

SECTION 1

DO YOU LOVE ME?

MAKING YOUNG PEOPLE OUR PRIORITY

Chapter 1

LOVE *RESPONDS*
EXAMINING THE CHALLENGE BEFORE US

Challenges require a response, and the church is facing a *true challenge*: young people in America and Europe are leaving the Christian church at an unprecedented rate.

I (J. Warner) first noticed the problem when I was a youth pastor. I took over leadership from my energetic, young predecessor, who had grown the group into a robust, engaged collection of junior high and high school students. Many had been raised together in the church, and they invited their friends to join the group. As a result, our students had deep relationships that bound them together.

In my first year as their pastor, I leaned heavily on my training as an artist (I have a BA in design and an MA in architecture). Our meetings were interactive, artistic, and experiential, incorporating music, imagery, and other sensory elements. The students seemed to enjoy the approach, and over time the group grew even larger.

But our results were *terrible*.

SOMETHING TIMELY

A recent study found that nearly 95 percent of teenagers in America have access to a smartphone.[1]

In the past, young people encountered skepticism primarily from their friends or from professors in the university.

Today, the internet is easily accessed on smartphones and mobile devices, bringing the most ardent skepticism home to the next generation at a very young age.

For this reason, we should expect the objections from young people to be far more articulate and well researched. Our responses must meet the challenge offered by internet skeptics, and we must start training our youth earlier than ever before.

Not long after graduating the first seniors, we found that most of them walked away from Christianity in the initial weeks of their freshman year at college. Many of our current students were still in touch with these new non-believers, and when I heard that they now rejected the existence of God, I was crushed, and I accepted the blame.

In the year since becoming their pastor, I had come to *love* these students. I felt a paternal responsibility to them. Like the apostle John, I wanted "no greater joy than this, to hear of my children walking in the truth" (3 John 1:4 NASB). When I heard that most of my graduating seniors had strayed from the family, I reconciled myself to the fact that I hadn't adequately prepared them for life after youth group. I thought, *I must be the worst youth pastor ever*. Then I started to study the issue more deeply and found that I wasn't alone.

If you're a youth pastor, Christian educator, or parent, I bet you've got a story of your own about a young ex-believer you love who was raised in the church. We've all got a student, son, daughter, grandson, granddaughter, niece, or nephew who has walked away from the truth. This isn't just an anecdotal problem. It's a national crisis. And it's also *personal*. Everywhere we travel, we hear heartbreaking stories from caring adults who know young people who have abandoned their faith. It can be especially hard when these are *our own kids.*

We've collected the studies about this phenomenon for more than fifteen years. Here are five things we've learned from the data:[2]

THE GROUP IS LARGE

The youngest generation in America is quickly becoming the *largest* generation in America. Born between 2000 and 2015, school-aged Christians are part of what has been termed "Generation Z" (aka, "Gen Z"). Other popular titles include "Post Millennials," "The App Generation," "The Selfie Generation," "Homelanders," and "iGen." You may have some of these young people in your own family. If not, they're certainly in your church and community. More importantly, Gen Z is projected to very quickly become the largest demographic group in the world (comprising 32 percent of the global population)[3] and is already the single largest media audience in the nation.[4] There's a reason

IF YOU'RE A PARENT
ASK A FEW QUESTIONS

 We sometimes take the spiritual growth of our kids for granted. Although they may continue to attend church with us, they may be far less committed to (or interested in) Christianity and also be reluctant to share their concerns and doubts.

Begin asking important questions, even at an early age:

• "What do you think is the most difficult thing to believe about Christianity?"

• "Of all the things the pastor said today, what seemed the most difficult to believe?"

• "What is your biggest question or doubt about Christianity?"

• "What do your skeptical friends say about Christianity?"

These are good questions because they are "open" questions (they can't be answered with a short "yes" or "no"), and they can serve to launch deeper conversations.

Don't rush to respond. Instead, be a good listener and use the data you collect to structure and inspire your own studies. And be sure to communicate in both your words and your body language that you are okay with their questions and doubts.

Make a list of the questions you want to be able to answer for your kids and begin to research the answers in preparation for your next conversation.

why the church needs to address the youngest members of our family. They outnumber us, and they are our future.

THE PROBLEM IS REAL

Gen Z has become the embodiment of an important (and disturbing) trend. Recent surveys and studies reveal that Gen Z is the least religious of all generations in America. In fact, "the percentage of teens who identify as atheist is double that of the general population."[5] This data is consistent with recent historical data. The number of young people leaving the church over the past twenty years is *staggering*. According to one study at UCLA, 52 percent of college students reported frequent church attendance the year before they entered college, but only 29 percent continued frequent church attendance by their junior year.[6] A variety of studies report that 50 to 70 percent of young Christians walk away from the church by the time they are in their college years.[7] Even those who don't leave find themselves struggling to believe Christianity is true. Approximately 40 to 50 percent of students in youth groups struggle in their faith after graduation.[8]

THE REASONS ARE REVEALING

Researchers have been asking young ex-Christians *why* they leave the church, and their answers are enlightening. Here are the most popular student responses from four different studies:

> "Some stuff is too far-fetched for me to believe."
> "Too many questions that can't be answered."[9]

"I'm a scientist now, and I don't believe in miracles."

"I learned about evolution when I went away to college."

"There is a lack of any sort of scientific or specific evidence of a creator."

"I just realized somewhere along the line that I didn't really believe it."

"I'm doing a lot more learning, studying, and kind of making decisions myself rather than listening to someone else."[10]

"Because I grew up and realized it was a story like Santa or the Easter Bunny."

"As I learn more about the world around me and understand things that I once did not, I find that the thought of an all-powerful being to be less and less believable."

"I realized that religion is in complete contradiction with the rational and scientific world, and to continue to subscribe to a religion would be hypocritical."

"It no longer fits into what I understand of the universe."[11]

"I have a hard time believing that a good God would allow so much evil or suffering in the world."

"There are too many injustices in the history of Christianity."

"I had a bad experience at church with a Christian."[12]

Do you see what we see? Most of these responses involve some form of *unanswered, intellectual skepticism*. Young believers struggle to answer tough questions from a Christian perspective. In addition to the intellectual doubts listed here, young ex-believers also cite hypocrisy and bad behavior on the part of fellow Christians. Young people are seeking a reasonable worldview that makes sense of reality.

THE DEPARTURE IS EARLY

While it's tempting to believe that secular universities—influenced by the natural sciences—are the sole reason young believers walk away from the church, the data doesn't support this claim. Most young people abandon their Christian faith while they are *still at home with their parents*. Today, incoming college freshmen, when surveyed *before* they enter college, are *three times* more likely to report that they are religiously unaffiliated than freshmen who entered college in 1986. Seventy-nine percent of these young people say they walked away from Christianity during their adolescent and teen years.[13] Many reported that they left the faith between the ages of ten and seventeen.[14]

THE FUTURE IS STILL BRIGHT

Despite the ominous findings of recent studies, young people who leave Christianity aren't necessarily leaving *God*. Eighty-eight percent of Americans report believing in *some kind* of God, higher power, or spiritual force, even if that being is not the God of the Bible.[15] Even among those who now claim *no* religious affiliation, known as "nones," 17 percent still say they believe in the God as described in the Bible, and 53 percent say they believe in a higher power or spiritual force. Even 18 percent of self-proclaimed *atheists* say they believe in some kind of higher, spiritual power. Young people who leave the church are still interested in spiritual things. They're *not* lost causes. They are willing to listen if we will listen *first*.

In fact, the act of *listening* is at the core of the solution. Looking at the data, one might conclude that the church simply needs to do a better job of teaching truth and making the case for Christianity, but that's only *part* of the answer. Young people are seeking reasonable explanations and *authentic relationships*; these are the two inseparable rails that will lead us toward a solution.

A BIBLICAL WAY FORWARD

As a first-year youth pastor, I (J. Warner) focused solely on relationships and

IF YOU'RE A YOUTH PASTOR OR MINISTER
PRESENT A FEW QUESTIONS

Youth group can be an intimidating place for students to ask questions or reveal what they really think about Christianity, especially if we haven't cultivated a ministry that embraces doubt.

When I (J. Warner) was a youth pastor, I met with my students on Sundays and then one additional weeknight in the home of one of our youth leaders. A home environment allowed us to soften the context for our discussions and strengthen our sense of "family."

During these weeknight meetings, we implemented a "You Ask It Bag." It was simply a large paper shopping bag in which students could place their questions, anonymously, about anything they wanted answered.

The bag was ever present at our meetings, and during the second half of each session, we would gather around the bag and begin drawing out questions. The bag accomplished two goals. First, it allowed students to ask questions safely. Second, it provided an incentive for our youth workers and volunteers to prepare themselves with good answers.

If you decide to use this approach, you might want to "seed" the bag with some of the common objections we've listed in this chapter so students who may be hesitant to voice their skepticism openly can hear an adequate response. In any case, the questions your students are asking can be used to plan future messages.

experiences. As I mentioned, I inherited an interactive group with deep, personal connections and friendships, and I feared they wouldn't accept me as the newcomer. So I spent months creating weekend events with the goal of deepening my relationship with each student. Each Sunday meeting provided students with plenty of interaction time. I'll be honest, I was more concerned about one question than any other: "Will they like me?"

Within months, I had gained their trust and confidence, but my focus on artistic experiences and relationships was *not* enough. I errantly believed that if they were still coming every week, they must think Christianity is true. As it turned out, some were just showing up because it was a safe place to hang out with people who loved them.

Relationships are incredibly important. University of Southern California sociology professor Vern Bengtson has commissioned a massive study on religious faith transmission since 1970. It involves four-generation families of more than 3,500 grandparents, parents, grandchildren, and great-grandchildren. Regardless of the particular religion, he has found that a warm relationship with the parents, and in particular the father, is the single most important factor in faith transmission. He also has discovered that healthy relationships with grandparents and the wider religious community are important for faith transmission.[16]

It is hard to overstate the importance of relationships. When I (Sean) taught high school full time, I worked diligently to build relationships with my students. I attended sporting events. My wife and I went to school dances. I looked to have conversations with students outside the classroom. And I took students on mission trips. I even participated in a school play!

But here is the reality: *kids need more than relationships.* Relationships alone are not enough. Christian students will find non-Christian, safe places to hang out once they get to the university. If it's only about relationships, you can expect students to find a community that will allow them to chase their passions without limitation or condemnation, especially if they've already decided Christianity isn't true. In fact, their desire to chase their passions may be the driving factor in their decision to reject Christianity. That's what many of us are inclined to do as fallen, sinful humans.

But make no mistake about it, truth alone is not enough *either.* Factual claims about God (or anything else for that matter) can sound like little more than "Blah, blah, blah" if they are delivered apart from an authentic relationship with someone who truly cares about you. Theology and apologetics can seem empty if we don't connect truth to how we live.

God calls us to truth *and* relationship. He possesses and demonstrates the perfect balance between justice and mercy, law and grace. If we want to impact students and teach them the truth about Christianity, we need to do our best to participate in this divine, relational balancing act. This is the approach the apostle Paul took. He shared not only the gospel with the Thessalonians but also *his very own life* (1 Thessalonians 2:8).

At our speaking engagements and community events, we are often approached by parents who sense their kids are starting to drift from their Christian foundation. We are regularly asked,

IF YOU'RE A CHRISTIAN EDUCATOR
POLL YOUR STUDENTS

Even in Christian schools, the spectrum of belief and certainty can be surprisingly broad. Some of your students are likely to have questions like the ones uncovered in the studies we've examined.

Depending on the relationship you've developed with your students, invite them to raise questions during one of your classes. If it's early in your semester—before you've had the chance to develop trust—ask them to submit their questions anonymously. Consider asking for responses to such topics as: "If you could ask God one question, what would it be?" or "If you could ask God to explain one confusing thing, what would it be?"

Make a list of the questions you receive, and work as a group to organize them into similar categories. Next, devote a section of your whiteboard or chalkboard to publicly remember the questions.

During your semester together, do your best to answer the inquiries directly, and refer to the list whenever a topic arises that fits into one of the categories.

As you're publicly recognizing and charting the questions, acknowledge the validity of investigating in the first place. Let your classroom be a place where these kinds of questions and discussions are welcome.

"What book can I give to my son (or daughter) to help them answer their questions about Christianity?" Books are great, and we've written our share, but unless you're willing to read them together with your kids or students (and they, too, are willing to read along), books can only provide truth *without* a personal relationship.

The better question might be, "What do *I* need to know to help my daughter (or son) answer the questions they have about Christianity? What do *I* need to do to strengthen the relationships I have with my kids so I can continue to speak into their lives and become the kind of person they want to engage with on these issues?" When we encourage parents to become the best Christian apologists their kids will ever know, we do so because we understand the connection between truth and relationships. Given this reality, here are a few suggestions based on the data we've already described:

MAKE A COMMITMENT

Let the statistics related to Gen Z and their departure from the church sink in a bit. Allow the sobering numbers to ignite a fire in your soul. God has a role for each of us in this time of crisis, even though He is still in complete control. We are called to *respond*. The apostle Paul understood a similar calling when he wrote his letter to the Colossians. He knew he would have to sacrifice his comfort and his desires to accomplish a greater work. To serve the church as a leader, minister, and steward, he committed himself to the mission: "For this purpose also I labor, striving according to His power, which mightily works within me" (Colossians 1:29 NASB). Each of us, in our own small way, can contribute to the important work of raising the next generation of Christians if we will simply *commit ourselves* to the task.

START EARLY

According to the statistics, young Christians decide to abandon the church long before they ever tell anyone and usually before they leave the homes of their parents. Polls continue to show that most people in America will become Christian *prior* to the age of fifteen. In fact, one large evangelical study found that the median age of conversion was *eleven*.[17] Why are older teens and young adults less likely to become Christians? If their own answers tell us anything, it's based on their intellectual skepticism, and the age of doubt and cynicism appears to be *dropping*. That's why it's so important for us to start *early*—even before your kids are verbalizing their questions. Moses instructed the Israelites to include children in their midst when talking about (or celebrating) God "so that they may hear and learn and fear the LORD your God" (Deuteronomy 31:12 NASB). It's tempting to think your church's high school youth ministry can eventually address the issues we've described, but the data tells a different story. We must start much earlier.

TAKE ON THE TOUGH ISSUES

Take another look at some of the responses offered by young people in the studies we've cited. Imagine getting some of these questions from the young Christians in your life:

> "What scientific proof do you have that God exists?"
>
> "Why should I believe in miracles?"
>
> "If evolution is true, why should I believe in God?"
>
> "Why should I trust something on 'faith' when I could use 'reason'?"
>
> "Why should I trust what you or my pastor has to say about Christianity?"
>
> "How is believing in God any different from believing in Santa Claus or the Easter Bunny?"
>
> "Why does science seem to contradict the claims of Christianity?"
>
> "Why would an all-powerful, all-loving God allow so much evil in the world?"
>
> "How can I be sure Jesus really rose from the grave?"
>
> "If Christianity is true, why are so many Christians hypocrites?"

"Why is the history of Christianity filled with so much violence?"

"Why should I care about any of this to begin with?"

Are you ready to answer these difficult questions? Most of us *aren't*. But the data tells us that these are *precisely* the kinds of questions we need to be prepared to answer if we want to help young people find the truth and follow the Savior. Don't let these difficult questions intimidate you. God is bigger than any of these objections, and each question listed here *can* be answered. Jesus told His followers to be courageous in the face of far greater oppression and resistance (read Matthew 10:16–20). How much more confident should we be that the Spirit of our Father will speak through us if we are willing to discuss the toughest issues?

BE PATIENT

I (J. Warner) wasn't raised in a Christian home. I was thirty-five years old before I set foot in an evangelical church for anything other than a wedding or a funeral. If you would have known me just one month prior to that

SOMETHING TIMELESS

The apostle Peter told his readers:

"But in your hearts honor Christ the Lord as holy, always being prepared to make a defense to anyone who asks you for a reason for the hope that is in you; yet do it with gentleness and respect" (1 Peter 3:15).

Peter encouraged his readers to defend the *truth*, but he did so in the context of *relationship*. We're commanded to answer the person who is asking the question, rather than simply answer the *objection* being offered. That's why Peter told his readers to be gentle and respectful. These characteristics of engagement are both relational *and* tactical. They help us build healthy relationships from which truth can be proclaimed, and they set the stage so that if we "are slandered, those who revile [our] good behavior in Christ may be put to shame" (verse 16).

The connection between truth and relationship is timeless.

time, you would have said, "Man, that Jim Wallace will *never* become a Christian." I was sarcastic and adamant about my position as an atheist. Yet here I am today, part of the Christian family. When Peter wrote, "The Lord is not slow about His promise, as some count slowness, but is patient toward you, not wishing for any to perish but for all to come to repentance" (2 Peter 3:9 NASB), he could have been writing about *me*. My personal experience of transformation has given me great patience with my own children. While I understand the urgency of the gospel, I also understand the timing of God.

I (Sean) learned this lesson of patience when a former student came back to sit in my high school apologetics class. It surprised me because this young man, when he was a senior in high school, asked me the minimal work he needed to do to get a C- so his parents would pay for his car insurance. He seemed to care little about the class. Then why was he back visiting? While attending a local junior college, some of his professors directly challenged his beliefs about God, creation, and the historical Jesus. I asked him if there was anything I could have done differently when he was in high school to better motivate and prepare him, and I will never forget his response. He nonchalantly said, "No. I simply wasn't there spiritually. I had to graduate and be challenged before I realized how important it is. But I was listening more than you probably think."

Be patient with yourself if you don't seem to have all the right answers or if the young people you're leading don't seem to be progressing as quickly as you might like. Just do your job. Study to be approved. Speak the truth. Love young people. The rest is in God's timing.

STAY BALANCED

Finally, recognize the fact that several of the responses from young people are centered on broken relationships (i.e., "I had a bad experience at church with a Christian"). When people don't believe something we know to be true, it's easy to lean more toward the *proclamation of truth* rather than toward the *building of relationships*. Don't give in to that inclination. The apostle Paul wrote to Timothy and commanded him to defend the truth and to "instruct certain men not to teach strange doctrines" (1 Timothy 1:3 NASB). But Paul understood the delicate balance between truth and love, doctrine and relationship. He told Timothy that the "goal of our instruction is love from a pure heart and a good conscience and a sincere faith" (1 Timothy 1:5 NASB). Our instruction—especially toward those who are younger—is a vehicle for truth, fueled by loving relationships. Our challenge is to avoid tilting our approach too far in either direction.

It shouldn't surprise us that the secret to Christian education is based on this connection between truth and relationships. The psalmist wrote that the entirety (the sum) of God's Word is *truth* (Psalm 119:160), and Jesus described Himself as *the truth* (John 14:6–7). Truth, from a Christian perspective, emanates,

SOMETHING TIMEWORTHY

What idea (or ideas) most resonated with you as you read this chapter? What concepts are worthy of consideration?

Idea(s):

_____

_____

_____

With whom could you (or *should* you) share this concept or information?

Person you have in mind:

_____

_____

_____

therefore, from a triune God who has been in relationship (with the Son and the Holy Spirit) for all eternity. And He enters into the human race to have a relationship with each one of us (John 17:3). So, as you read this book, remember that our model for teaching apologetics and Christian worldview is anchored and rooted in a uniquely Christian approach that unites truth to relationship, law to grace, justice to mercy.

Chapter 2

LOVE *UNDERSTANDS*
RECOGNIZING THE UNIQUENESS OF THIS GENERATION

I (Sean) grew up with parents on Cru staff (formerly Campus Crusade for Christ). Because my parents are well known and have built relationships with people in Cru over a number of decades, other staff members regularly ask me how my parents are doing. And I am more than happy to oblige them.

One time as a high school student, when I was at Cru Staff Training in Fort Collins, Colorado, a staff member named Mike asked how I was doing personally. Assuming he really wanted to know about my parents, I proceeded to tell him what they were up to. But he cut me off mid-sentence and said, "I'm not asking about your parents. I am interested in *you*. How are *you* doing? Tell me about *your story*." It caught me off guard. And I soon realized he was totally sincere. He was interested in knowing about my interests, dreams, and goals and not simply because of who my parents were. He was interested in understanding *me*.

Looking back over my years as a Cru staff kid, Mike had a big influence on my life. He invited me to weekend retreats and various events, and he always made a point to connect with me personally. One of the big reasons he was able to speak into my life was because he began by desiring to understand me as a person. Rather than importing assumptions from my family, my age, or where I was from, he made it clear that he wanted to understand me as a person.

When we truly love someone, we aim to understand that person. The challenge is that it takes time and effort. This is not only true for friends, neighbors, and coworkers, but it is especially true for the next generation of young people. If we truly want to love them, we must make the commitment to understand them first.

Proverbs 24:3 says, "By wisdom a house is built, and by understanding it is established." God's wisdom is certainly required to build a lasting, healthy home. But there must also be mutual understanding of one another. If you want a home, team, or youth group with meaningful relationships, it must begin with understanding.

More than a few times my (Sean's) father has told me, "It is more important to understand than to be understood." We often approach this generation and demand they understand us first. After

SOMETHING TIMELESS

Knowledge helps us understand people, so we can better love them. But knowledge is also power. My (Sean's) father often says, "A problem well defined is half-solved." Once we clearly understand the task at hand—by having the *knowledge*—we are in a much better position to find a reasonable solution.

First Chronicles 12:32 says the men of Issachar had "understanding of the times" in order to "know what Israel ought to do." In other words, they had *knowledge* of the times in which they lived in order to act with wisdom. Understanding the uniqueness of Generation Z helps us love them, but it also helps us guide them appropriately according to knowledge. Love and wisdom both require understanding.

all, we're the authority! But let's humble ourselves and aim to understand *before* being understood. Isn't this what Jesus calls us to do?

Even though it takes time to truly understand each young person you seek to impact, it's possible to ease your learning curve a bit if you do a little research *in advance*. During my deployment as a police officer, I (J. Warner) spent two years as an investigator in our agency's gang detail in Los Angeles County, and when I first accepted the position, I was afraid I was already too old—and too out of touch—to interact effectively with the gang members I encountered on the street. I didn't know their language, their personal histories, or much of their culture. My partner, on the other hand, had been serving on the team for over a year. He was much younger and grew up in neighborhoods that were far closer to the gang territories we patrolled. I knew I had to catch up and do it quickly if I wanted to engage this challenging group of young people.

IF YOU'RE A CHRISTIAN EDUCATOR
POLL YOUR STUDENTS

 If you teach at a Christian high school, this activity will help you better understand your students. Simply ask the questions below, or ones like them, and record their answers on the board. Let them know your goal is to understand them more clearly so you can better relate to them:

- What characteristics best describe your generation?

- Who are the most influential voices to your generation (i.e., YouTubers, artists, athletes, etc.)?

- What makes your generation different from previous generations?

- What are the most common misunderstandings older generations have about you?

- What are the collective experiences that help define your generation?

- What is hardest about being a young person today?

- What makes students in our school unique from those in other schools?

- If you could give leaders advice, what would it be?

When the activity is done, ask if you can share these insights with other teachers, staff members, administrators, and parents. Assure them that you will not reveal individual answers, but that you simply want to share key trends. If possible, you may do this in a few classes to get a broader sample. And if you take our advice, please consider sending it to us. We would love to see what your students come up with!

I started by attending every organized gang meeting I could find in Los Angeles County. I listened carefully to what other gang officers had experienced and learned over the years. I became a *sponge*, soaking up as much expertise and life experience as I could from men and women who had been interacting with gang members for nearly a decade. Once I got in the field, I leaned on the expertise of others for a year before I could finally draw on my own experiences and observations.

Our goal in this chapter is to offer you some expertise you can lean on as you begin to interact with the next generation. We have read hundreds of articles, dozens of books, and had countless conversations with students. Based on this expertise and research, we want to highlight some key trends that can help you best minister to this generation by understanding their unique beliefs, practices, and approaches to the world.

HOW WELL DO YOU KNOW THESE YOUNG PEOPLE?

How well do you know the Gen Z people in your life? How much have you interacted with them? Take a minute to complete a brief exercise with us. Think about the Gen Z students and children you know and write down the first three to four words that come to mind (without looking ahead to the end of the chapter) as you do your best to describe them:

_____

_____

_____

_____

Now keep this list of attributes in mind as we begin to describe the attributes of Generation Z. It is tempting to think that trends among Millennials (those born between 1981 and 1999) will apply to Gen Z. While there are some similarities, this assumption is deeply flawed. Some trends have carried over to the next generation, as we will see, but there are some stark differences too. Here is the bottom line: *if we are going to genuinely reach young people, we must have an accurate understanding of what they think, see, and how they feel about the world.*

Consider the defining events that characterize a generation. For instance, **Baby Boomers** (1946–1964) were formed deeply by the Vietnam War and the assassination of John F. Kennedy. **Gen Xers** (1965–1980) tend to remember the *Challenger* explosion, the tearing down of the Berlin Wall, and the AIDS crisis. **Millennials** (1981–1999) were probably shaped most profoundly by 9/11. These collective experiences deeply influence how members of each generation see their place in the world.

Gen Z also has some collective experiences that help define them. For instance, in many ways, Gen Z is a post-9/11 generation. They are the first generation without any memory of September 11 and were raised in a world still coming to grips with the reality of terrorism and what that means for immigration, government over-sight, and so on. Older members of Gen Z will recall the economic crash of 2008 and natural disasters, such as earthquakes in Haiti. Younger Gen Zers grew up practicing drills for the possibility of a school shooting.

Before we look at some unique factors about Gen Z,[1] let's compare these insights to our own experiences for a little perspective:

- Ronald Reagan is as distant for them as Dwight Eisenhower was for their parents.
- Email is an antiquated and useless technology to them.
- YouTubers are the new stars.
- With map apps on their smartphones, they have never needed directions.
- They consider the bands Nirvana and Guns N' Roses to be classic rock.

Times have clearly changed. Let's step out of our comfort zones and try to understand how Gen Z sees the world so that we can love them uniquely for who they are. Researchers studying Gen Z typically list several important observations and findings about this segment of our Christian family:

THEY'RE DIGITAL NATIVES

Gen Zers spend nearly every waking hour of the day interacting with some form of digital technology. This shapes their sleeping habits, how they process information, how they build and maintain relationships, and how they spend their spare time. The internet has been available and accessible to them since they were born. Gen Z is the first generation raised swiping screens on tablets and smartphones before they could even speak. While Millennials were raised on smartphones, only Gen Z was raised by parents (Gen X and Millennials) who were *also* on smartphones. The use of digital technology—and in particular social media—is perhaps the defining characteristic of this generation.

THEY'RE RESEARCHERS

Because Gen Z is continually connected to the internet, they're avid and skilled researchers. They know precisely where to go, across a variety of social media, news, or information platforms, to research any variety of topics, and they can do so very quickly. As a result, they understand how to educate themselves and find their own answers. According to surveys, 33 percent of Gen Zers watch online lessons, 20 percent read textbooks on tablets, and 32 percent work with classmates online.[2] Gen Zers can fact-check their parents (during conversations) and their youth pastors (during a message). They want to know the answers. And they have been raised in a world where the answer is just one click, or tap, away.

THEY'RE VISUAL MULTITASKERS

Eighty-nine percent of Gen Zers own a smartphone, and many own one by the time they are thirteen.[3] The most popular social media apps they use on these phones? Snapchat, Instagram, and YouTube—three entirely visual, video (or image) based platforms. In fact, 85 percent of Gen Zers visit YouTube more than any other social media platform.[4] They're also able to divide their attention repeatedly by multitasking between visual platforms. Eighty-four percent report multitasking on an internet-enabled device while watching television,[5] and Gen Zers have access to more opportunities to view visual materials (i.e., smartphones, televisions, laptops, desktops, and tablets) than any prior generation.

THEY'RE IMPATIENT

Gen Zers have been raised in an age in which speed and convenience rule the day. Streaming video platforms like Netflix have eliminated the need to wait to watch the next episode of your favorite show, streaming music apps have created immediate access to your preferred music, and online merchandise sites with seemingly endless choices of goods have removed the inconvenience of having to travel to the nearest store. Gen Zers expect instantaneous delivery on nearly everything from information to music to goods. Maybe that's why some studies place the attention span of Gen Zers at around eight seconds.[6] Internet industries understand this reality and have responded accordingly; Snapchat's ten-second story limit and YouTube's six-second pre-roll ads are just two examples.

SOMETHING TIMELY

Gen Z is growing up in a world changing more quickly than ever before. We have carefully researched this chapter and tried to root all our conclusions in empirical data and personal experience, but the reality is that these trends can change *overnight*.

We hope you will continue to read books, articles, and watch videos to understand this generation. As difficult as it can be, we must always be willing to adapt our approach to the unique needs of young people. We must never think, *This is the way I have always done things, and it has worked fine so I don't need to change.* The moment we stop trying to improve in our understanding of young people, we greatly diminish our relevance in their lives. For the sake of Gen Z, commit to continued learning, growth, and adaptation to their perspectives.

THEY'RE RACIALLY DIVERSE

There is more ethnic and racial diversity within Gen Z than any previous American generation, as this is the last generation in which most of the American population will be Caucasian. The first African-American president in US history was in office for eight of their formative years, and between 2000 and 2010, the Hispanic population grew at four times the rate of the total population.[7] While some Gen Zers may live in less ethnically diverse communities, they're still able to experience diversity in an unprecedented manner through social media, making this an unmistakable characteristic of Gen Z.

THEY'RE FLUID

Categories that were seemingly fixed and distinct for previous generations are now considered blurry, ambiguous, and *fluid* for Gen Z. Technology has contributed to a blurring of the lines between work and home, truth and fiction, fact and feeling, and our public

IF YOU'RE A YOUTH PASTOR OR MINISTER
SEEK TO UNDERSTAND YOUR STUDENTS

One of the biggest challenges, and greatest blessings, is knowing students personally. Why not invite your students to share their stories with you? At your next gathering, bring paper, pens, and envelopes. Play some music for ten minutes or so and suggest they spread out in the room, if that is more comfortable. Assure them their answers are for you only (hence, the sealed envelope). You might provide these prompts on a board or project them on a screen:

• Whether or not you believe in God, describe your faith story.

• If you could ask God one question, what would it be? Why?

• What can you share with me from your story to help me best understand who you are today?

You may want to encourage students who are more artistic to feel free to draw rather than write. The main idea is to get students sharing so you can better know them. If this is a new exercise, you might be surprised how much some students are willing to talk about their lives when given the chance to write their reflections. If you typically break into small discussion groups, then students may choose to write to you or their small group leader. Consider writing students a personal letter in response, letting them know that you are praying for them and available anytime (talk or text).

and private lives. Perhaps nowhere is there greater fluidity than with issues of sex, gender, and family. Young people today have grown up with the reality of single parents, stay-at-home dads, couples choosing not to have kids, cohabitation, three-parent families, and same-sex marriages. Few believe there is such a thing as a "normal" family. Only half of teens today believe gender is defined by one's sex at birth. Roughly one in eight Gen Zers describe their sexual orientation as something other than heterosexual.[8] And three in ten report personally knowing someone, most often a peer, who has changed his or her gender identity.[9] Formerly fixed categories of gender have increasingly broken down in the minds of Gen Z.

THEY'RE SOCIAL JUSTICE ORIENTED

Their outlook on racial and sexual diversity motivates Gen Z to engage specific kinds of causes and movements. Unlike prior generations that embraced anti-establishment causes (i.e., Baby Boomers) or environmental causes (i.e., Millennials), Gen Zers are motivated by causes surrounding *human equality*. These include issues related to poverty, human trafficking, refugees, and more. Gen Zers want to make a difference in their world: 60 percent want to use their jobs to make an impact, and 26 percent of sixteen- to nineteen-year-olds volunteer for causes they support.[10]

THEY'RE PRAGMATIC

Gen Zers have a realistic outlook on life. Their parents likely had a harder time financially than their grandparents, and Gen Zers experienced the 2008 recession firsthand as youngsters. In addition to a difficult economy, they've seen the growth of global terrorism and the increase of violence on school grounds here in America. Fifty-eight percent of Gen Zers are worried about the future.[11] They are *cautious* and pragmatic. Compared to prior generations, for example, they are less likely to drink underage and more likely to wear their seat belts.[12]

THEY'RE OVERWHELMED

In a cover story for *Time* magazine, a teenager named Faith-Ann described how overwhelmed young people today often feel: "We're the first generation that cannot escape our problems at all. We're all like little volcanoes. We're getting this constant pressure, from our phones, from our relationships, from the way things are today."[13] More than two out of three teens today feel overwhelmed by everything they need to do each week.[14] Previous generations could usually get away from bullying or peer pressure, at least in part. But with social media, young people find it increasingly difficult—if not impossible—to escape their troubles. The corresponding stress and anxiety, coupled with the constant bombardment of information, can be overwhelming.

THEY'RE LONELY

Based on their online presence, most teens seem eminently happy. But this happiness is often a veneer hiding *deep* loneliness. In fact, according to psychology professor Jean Twenge, this new generation is on the verge of the greatest mental health crisis in decades.[15] She noticed a significant increase in depression and loneliness around 2012, the year iGen (her term for Gen Z) became high school seniors.

And this trend crosses socioeconomic, racial, and demographic categories. She attributes the increased loneliness to the ubiquity of smartphones and the resulting decrease in personal interaction. Regardless of the cause, one thing is clear: there is a growing mental health crisis of loneliness and depression among today's students.

THEY'RE INDIVIDUALISTIC

Because of the explosion of consumerism in the 1960s, Baby Boomers are often referred to as Generation Me. A 2014 *Time* cover story referred to Millennials as the "Me Me Me Generation."[16] And this me-focused trend continues with Gen Z. They are arguably the Me, Me, Me, *Me* Generation. Whether in terms of religious choice, gender preference, or the basis for morality, young people today have grown up in a culture that places the individual as the highest authority. Gen Zers resist judging the moral choices of others, and individual feelings often trump facts.

THEY'RE TRANSPARENT

Authenticity is important to Gen Z. Given all the possible sources of information available to them online, they struggle to know who they can trust. They seek real relationships, and they respect transparency. They know people aren't perfect. Nearly 80 percent of Gen Zers, for example, prefer advertising that shows real people in real situations.[17] They are less impressed with slick presentations or false personas; they can detect exaggerations, inaccuracies, or prideful attitudes. The more transparent and vulnerable a speaker or teacher is, the more likely he or she will be trusted by Gen Zers. They want to hear personal stories that reveal imperfections and weaknesses, because they know *they* have similar vulnerabilities.

THEY'RE POST-CHRISTIAN

As we described in the last chapter, more young Americans describe themselves as religiously unaffiliated than ever before. The frequency of Bible reading, prayer, and church attendance is also declining. The Bible no longer holds the same authority in the minds of this generation, at least in terms of what previous generations *claimed* to believe. In her book *iGen*, Jean Twenge concluded, "The move away from religion is no longer piecemeal, small, or uncertain; it is large and definitive. More young Americans are thoroughly secular, disconnecting completely from religion, spirituality, and the larger questions of life."[18] A national study by the Barna Group in partnership with Impact 360 Institute found that only 4 percent of Gen Z has a biblical worldview.[19] But as we've noted, there are still opportunities to share spiritual truths with Gen Zers. According to a recent survey, many Gen Zers report that they view religious leaders as better role models than celebrities, professional athletes, or politicians.[20]

HOW WELL DO YOU INTERACT WITH THESE YOUNG PEOPLE?

Now that we've looked at some *timely* attributes common to Gen Z, let's take a moment to examine three *timeless* principles we can apply as we interact with them:

REMEMBER, EVERY YOUNG PERSON HAS A UNIQUE STORY

While there are significant cultural events, technological advancements, and trends that deeply shape a generation, we must remember that no one is simply a product of his or her generation. Every young person is different and unique. Social media, for example, is one of the defining characteristics of Generation Z. But we shouldn't assume that every single young person uses social media in the same manner or to the same degree. In fact, many young people (for a variety of reasons) don't use social media *at all*. The trends and characteristics we're describing in this book will help you understand the next generation, but remember: not all students fit generational stereotypes.

FOCUS ON WHAT WE HAVE IN COMMON

Because language, dress, entertainment, and technology change so rapidly, it is easy to feel disconnected from generations other than our own. But the reality is that we have much more in common than

IF YOU'RE A PARENT
ASK A FEW QUESTIONS

If your kids are Gen Zers, the research in this chapter will provide fresh perspectives. But you'll want to continue going deeper to understand their unique personalities and interests. Consider taking your kids out for coffee, ice cream, or a meal (possibly as you pick them up after school) and asking them these questions (or ones like them). Tell them you just want to listen so you can become a better mom or dad:

- If you had a free day to do anything, what would you do?
- What are your favorite memories of our family?
- How would you describe our family to an outsider?
- Are there some things other families do that you wish we did together?
- What are your favorite things to do with me?
- If you were me, what changes would you make to our family?
- Do you want to be a parent someday?
- Is there anything I do that frustrates you?
- What is one thing I could do to be a better dad (or mom) to you? >>

you might think, and the reason is simple: regardless of race, age, socioeconomic status, or any other secondary - factor, every human being is made in the image of God (Genesis 1:27). We all know right from wrong (Romans 2:14–16). We yearn for eternal life (Ecclesiastes 3:11).

>> The goal of these questions is to understand how your son or daughter sees your family and their place in it. Don't get defensive. Just listen with empathy and understanding. This will help show your willingness and desire to be a better parent. There is another reason this is important: Gen Zers highly value authenticity. They don't expect perfection, and they respond when we are real.

We love stories. We want to belong, to be loved, and to live significant lives. We yearn for meaningful relationships. This is true for Baby Boomers, Gen X, Millennials, and *every other* generation who ever has—or ever will—live. It's true for you, it's true for us, and it's true for every young person in your life. So, rather than focusing on *differences* across the generations, we hope you will focus primarily on what *binds us together*.

STAY POSITIVE

We started this section of the book asking you to write down the first words that came to mind when trying to describe Gen Zers. Now compare your description to the attributes we've offered. Are they similar? More importantly, did you choose words that are primarily *positive* or *negative*? We ask adults around the country to perform this exercise, and while many people use optimistic words to describe Gen Zers, it amazes us how many offer *pessimistic* descriptions like "lazy," "entitled," "gullible," and "selfish." For many people, these descriptions are the lens through which they understand and relate to this *entire* generation. If you see Gen Zers

SOMETHING TIMEWORTHY

What attributes of Gen Z
were most eye opening?

Attribute(s):

_____

_____

_____

_____

How might this new knowledge
change the way you approach the
young people in your life?

_____

_____

_____

_____

through a negative lens, how do you think you'll interact with them? That's why our third and final principle is simple: *be positive*. Are there reasons to be concerned about this generation? Yes. Are there positive things to celebrate? Of course. Be mindful of your concerns (and address them with wisdom), but don't dwell on the negative. Instead, rejoice over our kids and relish the opportunity to mentor, guide, teach, and love them.

We continually meet parents, youth pastors, and Christian teachers who express a common interest in the future of young Christians and a common love for the Christian community. We share this concern and passion. Together, let's strive to understand *timely* truths about Gen Z as we embrace and employ the *timeless* truth of Scripture.

Chapter 3

LOVE *RELATES*
CONNECTING WITH THE HEARTS OF YOUNG PEOPLE

"Dad, I'm not sure if I believe in Christianity. I want to know what is true, but I have a lot of questions."

What would *you* say if your son or daughter spoke these words to you? How would you respond if these words came from a young Christian you deeply cared about? Well, as a nineteen-year-old college student, I (Sean) spoke these words to my father, not knowing how he would respond, especially since I was questioning the very *message* he has committed his life to proclaiming.

And yet I will never forget my father's confident response: "Son, I am glad to see you exploring your faith seriously, because you can't live on my convictions. You have to know for yourself what you think is true. If you genuinely seek truth, I am confident you will follow Jesus, because He is the truth. Only walk away from what you have learned growing up if you conclude it is false. And know that your mom and I will love you no matter what you believe."

Not long ago, I decided to ask my dad how he was *really* feeling when I told him about my doubt years earlier, assuming he must have been deeply concerned at the time. Was he worried I might abandon my faith? What was actually going through his mind?

His response caught me off guard. He told me that he wasn't worried about my faith journey because of the depth of our *relationship*. While he believes the evidence for Christianity is compelling, it was our relationship that gave him confidence I would stay in the faith. There were certainly no guarantees, of course, and my dad is endlessly optimistic by nature, but his response illustrates a point we want to drive home in this book: *truth is best learned and sustained in relationship.*

If we want the next generation to come to know the faith, we have to teach, model, and incarnate truth in our relationship with them. It is not truth *or* relationship—it is truth *and* relationship.

SOMETHING TIMELY

The purpose of this chapter is to offer principles and strategies for building deep relationships with young people. At the same time, we hope you will strike a balance and allow them to appropriately fail.

Parents today have the tendency to be overly protective of their kids ("helicopter parenting"). Please remember—failure is not terminal. Every failure is an opportunity for a young person to grow. We must give young people the space to fail and learn from their failures, and then we must be present to walk them through it. Isn't that what God does for us?

And this is exactly what God has done for us. Rather than merely sending His message through a book, a prophet, or an angel, God came *Himself* to us through the person of Jesus Christ in both grace and truth (John 1:14). Jesus came down in human flesh so we could know *God* personally and have eternal life (John 17:3). Jesus traveled with His disciples. He ate with them. He ministered with them. He passed on truth relationally and calls us to do the same (Matthew 28:19–20). Our modern culture is radically different from the first century, but the principle remains the same—*we must relationally commit to passing on truth to the next generation.*

A LONELY GENERATION

As we saw in chapter 2, loneliness is a defining feature of young people, including Christians, today. Some studies even suggest Gen Z may be the loneliest generation.[1] A number of reasons account for this, many of which are tied to technology. With ever-present access to social media, young people have been raised to constantly compare their appearance and accomplishments to others, to fear missing out ("FOMO"), and to portray their lives as perfectly happy. These forces can be crushing to the self-image of a young person.

But we think the epidemic of loneliness goes even deeper. At the heart, *the loneliness of this generation stems from broken relationships.* Jesus said the greatest commandment is to *love* God and *love* other people (Mark 12:28–33). So many in this generation *hurt* because they lack the healthy relationships God has designed them to experience with both Himself and other people. Many are asking the questions, "Who am I?" "Where do I belong?" and "Does my life have any meaning?" without the relational anchor God has designed them to have.

When healthy relationships are lacking, young people experience a vacuum they will seek to fill with a relational counterfeit. This lonely generation will search for something to fill their relational hole, and our culture has many options that can easily become addictive.

To varying degrees, every generation of young people has sought to find their place in the world. But what is different for Gen Z is the depth of loneliness many feel *and* the availability of endless counterfeits that claim to be able to fill their hearts with meaning.

Let's consider some of the relational counterfeits vying for the hearts of Gen Z:

CONSUMERISM

Commercials, social media promotions, and celebrities promise this generation that if they just buy a certain product, their lives will be filled. They may not say this directly, of course, but the incessant exposure to advertisements sends young people the message that they are missing out and *need* a consumer item for fulfillment.

BUSYNESS

With social media, YouTube, television, and more, it is possible to never get bored. But *why* is this generation so busy and distracted? We suspect a big reason is that many do not want to feel their emotional hurt. They would rather keep it at bay. It is much easier to live in a state of distraction than to confront the loneliness in the human heart.

PORNOGRAPHY

Pornography is epidemic with young people. But *why* is it so prevalent? The combination of accessibility and teen hormones certainly plays a part. But we believe pornography fulfills a deeper relational need in a counterfeit way. How so? It removes vulnerability, which is necessary for real love. The teen boy, for instance, who struggles to relate to girls no longer needs to risk rejection by asking her out. He can feel good watching the smiling porn star who will never turn him away.

SOCIAL MEDIA

Social media can be a wonderful way to share ideas, learn new facts, and connect with like-minded people. But humans also need *embodied* relationships. We need appropriate touch, eye contact, and human presence. Social media can help foster human connection in a remarkable way, but it cannot replace our need for relationships. A *digital* "like" cannot replace a *physical* hug.

VIDEO GAMES

Video games can be a fantastic source of entertainment and connection. But they can also become a counterfeit that young people look to in order to fill their hearts with meaning and significance. Many video games are

IF YOU'RE A CHRISTIAN EDUCATOR
MAKE YOURSELF AVAILABLE

 We know you are busy with lesson plans, grading, extracurricular activities, and the other myriads of responsibilities teachers inherit. I (Sean) taught full time as a high school Bible teacher for a decade and can remember being assigned all sorts of tasks beyond the classroom.

Let us ask you a critical question: How available are you for your students? I was speaking at a private school in the Midwest and met a teacher who closes his door and window blinds during lunch and after school in order to grade papers. We understand busyness, but what message does this send to students? If you want to meaningfully speak truth into their lives, communicate through your words and actions your availability. Consider a few questions:

• Do you tell your students that you are available for help outside the classroom?

• Are you welcoming when students first enter the room?

• Do you know their names and use them?

• Do you leave your classroom during the day to connect with students around campus?

• Do you attend school functions, such as sporting events and plays, to convey that you value students?

• Do you express genuine interest in the lives of the students outside the class?

designed to subtly promise respect, community, identity, and control—the very things many youth are searching for.

Our point is not to disparage everything (except porn, which we think is *always* wrong). Consumer products can be beneficial. Video games can be fun and entertaining. There is a time for busyness. And we both regularly use social media to share the truth of Christianity. But before we get to practical steps for building relationships with young people, it is vital to understand the role that different counterfeits can play in their lives. We are all built for relationships, and when they are lacking, *something* will fill the void. Broken relationships are at the heart of why this generation has so many addictions.

RELATIONSHIPS SHAPE HOW WE VIEW GOD

As a young agnostic, my (Sean's) father was challenged to examine the historical claims of Christ. Before heading to law school, he set out to disprove the Christian faith. This was long before Google, and so he traveled internationally to Europe and the Middle East to visit libraries and museums, looking to gather the evidence he believed would disprove the claims of Christ.

But he ended up concluding that Christianity was in fact true. The evidence merely got his attention, though. His biggest barriers were relational and emotional. People would describe God as a heavenly Father and he would think, *Why would I want a heavenly Father when my* earthly *father is a drunk?* His relationship with his earthly father had deeply shaped how he viewed God. It was through an accurate understanding of the character of God as exemplified in Scripture, lived out relationally with other Christians, that he could grasp God's love and thus be drawn to the faith.

My father's experience fits what psychologist Paul Vitz refers to as the "theory of the defective father." The idea is that our relationship with our earthly father deeply affects how we view God. According to Vitz, if someone has a distant, harsh, or disappointing father, belief in a heavenly father becomes difficult (if not impossible). To make his case, Vitz points to prominent atheists who fit the profile, such as Bertrand Russell, Friedrich Nietzsche, Jean Paul Sartre, Albert Camus, and Karl Marx.[2] There are certainly exceptions. And people can have psychological reasons for believing in God. But overall, Vitz stresses how deeply psychological reasons—and in particular human relationships—shape how we view God.

TRUST: AN IRREPLACEABLE COMMODITY

Building relationships has always required trust. And trust is *especially* vital for relating to young people today. Because of mobile technology, Gen Zers are surrounded by never-ending voices vying for their hearts and minds. The question is—who are they going to trust?

If you are an older Baby Boomer, you remember exactly where you were when John F. Kennedy was shot. The

SOMETHING TIMELESS

It is a humbling thought that our character and our relationships with young people can shape their understanding of God. To varying degrees, they will view the character of God and the Christian life based on the significant Christian adults in their lives—*including each one of us*. We encourage you to consider two questions. First, how deeply is your own theology, and relationship with God, shaped by your human relationships, including the one with your father? Second, how significantly are your relationships shaping young people in your life? We hope these questions are a reminder to be on your knees in prayer asking God for love, humility, and wisdom so you can be a faithful role model for the next generation.

IF YOU'RE A YOUTH PASTOR OR MINISTER
MAKE SURE YOU HAVE THE FACTS

As we saw in chapter 2, members of Gen Z research everything. They have access to unlimited information at their fingertips and can check any story or claim you make in your teaching. Trust us, they will check the facts. I (Sean) remember the first time I spoke to a group of skeptics at Berkeley. They checked everything I said right on the spot and challenged me along the way. Even Christian kids do this regularly when we interact with them.

Thus, to build trust with this generation, it is more important than ever to get your facts right. If you get too many things wrong, you will lose credibility, and thus your voice, to genuinely influence this generation. And it may not happen until years later when students are in college. If you misrepresent historical or scientific facts, and students discover differently in the future, it can undermine how they view spiritual lessons. Consider a few questions:

- Do you do your homework in preparation for a lesson?

- When speaking on a subject, do you qualify the strength of your claims to the strength of the evidence?

- Do you offer alternative perspectives to your students and critique them fairly? >>

rest of us have seen a still photo or the infamous black-and-white video clip of him being shot in the back seat of a car. A handful of conspiracies have arisen around his death. Yet one of the underlying assumptions has been that if we had more information—such as more video cameras or pictures—we could have greater access to the truth.

Fast-forward to 9/11. We have vastly more camera angles and photos for planes hitting the buildings than for the JFK shooting. Yet, are there more conspiracies or fewer? Quite clearly there are *more*. The takeaway is that more information does not necessarily result in greater confidence in the truth. In fact, sometimes increased access to information leads to greater skepticism.

And this is what we find with Gen Z. As we saw in chapter 2, this is a digital generation that daily experiences information overload. Given how many perspectives there are on every issue, many in this generation wonder *what they can know* and *who they can trust*.

>> • Do you admit when you are not an expert on a topic and provide someone who is?

• Are you willing to admit when you are wrong?

There are two key ways to build trust with this generation. The first is knowledge. We listen to doctors because of their expertise about medicine and the human body. And we listen to our car mechanic because of his or her knowledge of cars. If we want young people to listen to us, we must *know* what we are talking about. We must give them a narrative—a worldview—to effectively navigate challenges that arise in our culture. We will explore this in greater depth in the next chapter.

The second way to build trust with this generation is through relationships. We need to earn the trust to communicate Christian truth to them in a genuine fashion. And that trust is earned through investing our time and energy in getting to know them as individuals. Before we consider specific steps for building relationships, keep in mind these three important principles for connecting with young people:

RELATIONSHIPS ARE NOT MERELY TOOLS FOR INSTRUCTION

It is easy to think of building relationships as a strategy to teach Christian truth. Gen Zers are strongly motivated by relationships: 75 percent do not want to let others down, and 75 percent want to make a difference for someone else.[3] Yet building relationships is not something we do merely to persuade them to adopt our beliefs, but because God has called us to love them as divine image bearers.

BUILDING RELATIONSHIPS BEGINS WITH US

Given that this generation has its own music, dress, language, and technology, it's less intimidating to wait for young people to take the initiative if they are interested in connecting with us. Yet this is a colossal mistake. The heart of a young person is to be known by a caring adult who believes and expresses: *You matter to me. I care about you. I will sacrifice to invest in your life to help you be all God has designed you to be.* We must be willing to take the initiative to build relationships with this generation.

CONNECTING REQUIRES UNDERSTANDING THEIR FRAME OF REFERENCE

Relational conflict often results from unexpressed assumptions. Thus, effective communication involves understanding where another is coming from. And this is particularly true for Gen Zers, who tend to have different assumptions than adults, especially about technology. For instance, many teens do not view it as rude to have a phone out during a conversation. Adults tend to differ. Can we at least aim to understand where they are coming from rather than responding with anger? Our point is simply that building relationships with members of Gen Z involves trying to see the world as they do and imagining *what it is like* to be a young person today. And keep in mind, seeing the world from their perspective does not necessarily mean you agree with their way of thinking.

TEN STRATEGIES FOR CONNECTING WITH GENERATION Z

Here are ten strategies we have found helpful in building relationships with young people. You don't have to do all of these. Start with *one*, and then try another. Over time, you will grow in your relationships with the Gen Zers in your life.

SHARE STORIES

There is a reason why Jesus told so many stories: we *love* stories, *relate* to stories, and *remember* stories. They shape how we view the world. And they allow us to be known by a young person. Describe special memories about your upbringing, your work, and your hobbies. Be vulnerable, and share both your successes and your failures. You don't have to tell your entire life story to a young person, but let him or her know you can relate by sharing relevant life experiences and struggles. This generation processes quickly, as we saw in chapter 2, and they are eager to entertain a personal story.

ENTER YOUR KIDS' WORLD

It is impossible to truly know young people until you enter their world. Watch their movie of choice. Listen to their music. Eat at a restaurant they enjoy. Play a video game with them. This not only shows that you value them but gives you a glimpse into their dreams and desires. Rather than merely inviting them into your world, go into theirs.

PRACTICE EMPATHY

Empathy is the ability and willingness to enter into the feelings of another. If we want to earn favor with young people, we need to give them permission to share their feelings with the security that we will not be quick to judge. Romans 12:15 says, "Rejoice with those who

IF YOU'RE A PARENT
IMAGINE A FEW SCENARIOS

Our kids will let us down. This is inevitable. But what we often fail to do is prepare ahead of time for how we might respond to their failures so we can minister to them biblically, and in love, when the time comes. For instance, have you considered these questions:

- What if my daughter gets pregnant?
- What if I discover one of my kids is looking at porn?
- What if my son is caught cheating on a test at school?
- How would I respond if I discovered one of my kids was smoking weed?
- What would I do if one of my kids sexted another student?
- How would I respond if my son or daughter bullied another student or is bullied by one?

These are the kinds of scenarios parents dread. But the only way we can respond with truth and grace is if we plan beforehand how we will react to this news if it comes. The goal is to respond lovingly and firmly so as to preserve the relationship but also guide our kids to authentic healing. Take a few moments and reflect on how you might respond in these situations. And talk to your spouse about them so you can implement a plan together.

rejoice, weep with those who weep." When young people are sad, share their sorrow. When they are happy, share their joy. Expressing empathy shows young people that we relate to them and recognize them as valuable human beings.

BE A GOOD LISTENER

James 1:19 says to "be quick to hear, slow to speak." As adults, we often get this backward—we are quick to speak and slow to hear. And yet for a distracted and impatient generation, listening can be one of our best ways to connect. Good listening says, "You are important to me. I want to understand you, so I can respond in a caring manner." Ask genuine questions. Give eye contact. Show empathy. And try to genuinely understand *before* you speak.

EXPRESS UNCONDITIONAL LOVE

When I (Sean) was a kid, my father was writing and speaking publicly about abstinence. Yet I was twelve years old and my hormones were kicking in. I remember thinking, if I became sexually active—*I could really blow it for my dad.* So I decided to ask him what would happen if I got a girl pregnant, and I will never forget what he said: "Son, I don't care if the whole world calls me a hypocrite; you and I will work it through together." This was one of the most meaningful ways my father communicated to me that his love was unconditional.

MENTOR A YOUNG PERSON

By suggesting you mentor a young person, we are not asking you to add another program to your schedule. Rather, ask yourself a simple question—*what am I already doing that I could include a young person alongside me?* Mentoring involves bringing a young person along with you on the tasks you already do anyways. It could be as simple as taking one of your students with you to the store or finding a young person who also enjoys working out. For me (Sean), I try to bring one of my kids, or a student from one of my classes, whenever I speak at a local event. It gives us a chance to be together and build a relationship.

SET REASONABLE BOUNDARIES

Even though Generation Z is individualistic, they actually want boundaries. According to one study in Britain, 69 percent of teens thought parental controls online were a good idea.[4] In another study, 54 percent of US teens wished they were better able to limit the amount of time they were on their phones, and over 60 percent would like to spend more time socializing face to face than online.[5] Reasonable boundaries communicate to this generation that we love them enough to protect them from harm (even though they will initially protest such boundaries). For instance, students need certain times and places without smartphones. Teachers can set reasonable boundaries in the classroom. Coaches can do so at practice. And parents must set reasonable boundaries in the home.

PRAY

One deep way to show a young person that you care is to pray for him or her. If you are counseling a young person, or just in a conversation, ask if it's okay if you pray for him or her. You might not have a solution for his or her problem, but it is easy to say, "I am not sure how to fix it either. But can I pray for you?"

SHARE A MEAL

Whenever I (J. Warner) arrest a suspect and prepare to interview him or her, I order a meal for *both of us*. I then sit down with my suspect, so we can eat *together*. When I first started doing this, my partner refused to join us. "I'll buy him a meal," he said. "But I refuse to eat with a killer!" I could certainly understand where my partner was coming from. But something remarkable happens over a shared meal. We don't typically eat with strangers or people we don't like. After becoming a Christian, I developed a heart for the suspects I arrested. I saw our meal together as the first step in a *relationship*, despite the tragic circumstances that brought us together. My interviews following these meals were markedly different from the interviews I conducted before I recognized the divine power of a shared meal. Think about it for a minute. How many important moments in Scripture occurred during a meal between God and His people?

The power of a meal is equally important for young people. The results are indisputable—kids who have regular meals with their family, or other caring adults, are less likely to engage in risky behavior and to perform better in school. It is over meals that stories are told, jokes are laughed at, and meaningful conversations occur. In a generation that is fluid, sharing regular meals creates a sense of identity, belonging, and community.

HAVE A CONVERSATION

The A&E channel ran a special show called *Undercover High*, in which seven young adults aged twenty-one to twenty-six went back to high school to get an inside perspective on students today. The undercover students made many of the same observations about Generation Z that we made in chapter 2, yet what alarmed them most was the disconnect between teens and adults. One of the undercover students said, "They [teens] are craving for adults to understand them and see them for who they are and the struggles they are facing."[6] The undercover students concluded that, most of all, young people today just want someone to talk to. Are you willing to have a conversation with a young person and help fill his or her deep need for relationship?

LOVE RELATES

There's a reason why the word *relate* is the root of the term *relationship*. If we hope to *relate* to the youngest generation, we have

SOMETHING TIMEWORTHY

Which relational strategy (or strategies) offered in this chapter seem most applicable, given your setting?

Strategy:

_____

_____

_____

What might this approach look like in your context?

_____

_____

_____

to invest in *relationships*. There is, perhaps, no better illustration of the importance of relationships than social media "comment" sections. I (J. Warner) have been making the case for Christianity and God's existence for many years now online, and during this time, thousands of people have commented on my articles, blog posts, videos, and podcasts. Some of these remarks have been courteous, and some have not. One pattern has emerged: the people with whom I have little or no personal relationship are by far the harshest critics of my work. If a friend disagrees with something I've written, he or she is more likely to provide a gracious counter-argument. Strangers, however, are less kind, patient, or well mannered. As a result, I'll confess that I'm less likely to take their criticism seriously, *even if it is warranted*.

Relationships are the runway on which truth lands. Take the time to listen with empathy, mentor from a place of wisdom, and demonstrate your concern and care for the young people you hope to influence. Prepare them for *truth* by gaining their *trust*.

Chapter 4

LOVE *EQUIPS*

GIVING KIDS A WORLDVIEW THAT BRINGS SIGNIFICANCE

Surfing looks easy. How hard can it be to stand on a board and ride down a wave? I (Sean) remember thinking this shortly before I went surfing the first time as a junior high student. My friends tried to warn me and prepare me for the challenges of learning how to surf, but I recall thinking, *No worries. I got this.*

Surfing may have looked easy, but I got totally pummeled that day. I couldn't even make it out to the break because I kept getting tossed and turned by the white water. Battered and bruised, I gave up sooner than I would like to admit.

Because my friends cared, they tried to equip me ahead of time for the challenges that lay before me. When danger is imminent, the loving thing to do is to both warn someone and help equip them for the approaching encounter. If this is true for learning to surf, it is markedly true when it comes to the challenges our students face in trying to navigate today's culture. If we love the youth of this world, we will take seriously the task of equipping them with the necessary tools so they can thrive in their faith.

WHY EQUIPPING YOUTH IS VITAL

As we have seen, there are a number of reasons young people choose to disengage with the church. But at its heart, the issue is a matter of worldview. In light of our research and experience, we believe the primary reason Gen Z disconnects from the church is our failure to equip them with a biblical worldview that empowers them to understand and navigate today's culture.

SOMETHING TIMELESS

Second Corinthians 10:3–5 says, "For though we walk in the flesh, we are not waging war according to the flesh. For the weapons of our warfare are not of the flesh but have divine power to destroy strongholds. We destroy arguments and every lofty opinion raised against the knowledge of God, and take every thought captive to obey Christ."

We are called to build relationships with this generation, but we are also called to "destroy arguments" raised up against the knowledge of God. As we help young people think biblically about all areas of life, they must learn how to reject false ideas that stand in the way of the gospel.

So many young Christians are ill prepared to face the moral, intellectual, relational, and spiritual challenges that confront them daily. They don't have an anchor to help ground them amid the cultural chaos, and as a result, many find their faith shipwrecked on the shores of our increasingly secular culture.

Here is a stark reality: if we do not consciously equip young Christians with a biblical worldview, they will unconsciously absorb the ideas of today's culture. And because of information overload, Gen Zers are exposed to more competing worldviews—and at earlier ages—than any generation in history.

In the last chapter, we talked about how important relationships are for building trust with a digital generation. But young people also need a worldview through which they can make sense of information bombardment. In this chapter, we explore the nature of worldview, unpack some unique worldview challenges we face in equipping this generation, and offer some practical steps for helping young people think and live *Christianly*.

WHAT IS A WORLDVIEW?

Worldview may sound like a fancy word. But when I (J. Warner) first started teaching students in my youth group, I described worldview as simply a view of the world that answers three critical questions: (1) How did we get here?—*Origin*; (2) Why is everything so messed up?—*Predicament*; and (3) How can we fix it?—*Resolution*.

Christianity, for example, provides the following answers: (1) We are the special creation of a Holy God, created in His image. (2) We are fallen, rebellious creatures living in an equally fallen universe that "groans and suffers the pains of childbirth" (Romans 8:22 NASB). Because we are sinful creatures, we are separated from God and often reject His guidance and violate His laws. The solution? (3) All creation will be restored and reunited with God through the saving work of Jesus Christ, who paid the price for our sin and offered forgiveness through His death on the cross.

Every worldview offers its own responses to these foundational questions, forming a belief system that also answers some of the *other* big questions:

- What is the purpose of human life?
- What kind of life brings genuine happiness?
- What is the basis of morality?
- Does God exist?
- Is there life after death?

It might be helpful to think of a worldview as a mental map of reality. Like a map that helps navigate physical terrain, a worldview is a mental map that helps navigate nonphysical reality. Yet, as helpful as this illustration can be, we want to be careful not to mitigate worldview simply to the thinking part of our being. Worldview is not just about the *mind*—it is also about the orientation of the *heart*. Simply put, a worldview is a fundamental commitment to reality that shapes how we live.

Everyone has a worldview. It is impossible not to be committed to a certain view of the nature of the world and make choices in light of that commitment. But there are some pressing questions many people have not deeply considered: What is my worldview? Why do I see the world as I do? Is it helping me navigate reality accurately? For many people—and especially young people—their worldview consists of untested assumptions and practices they have absorbed from the wider culture.

If we are going to help young people cultivate a Christian world-view, we need to consider what Gen Zers say they believe. Let us begin with asking some questions. Take a minute to guess what percentage of young people today hold the following beliefs, before you skip to the answers a few paragraphs below:

1. _____% Believe gender is how a person feels, not their birth sex.
2. _____% Believe happiness is defined by financial success.
3. _____% Believe lying is morally wrong.
4. _____% Believe science and church teachings are complementary.
5. _____% Believe many religions can lead to eternal life, as there is no one true religion.

Before we offer the correct percentages, have you considered how worldview connects from beliefs to behavior? For instance, if a young person believes that many religions lead to eternal life, then why live boldly as a follower of Jesus? If a young person believes science and church teachings are in conflict, who is he or she really going to consider the authority? If a young person believes happiness comes from financial success, then will he or she be able to embrace the Christian message of sacrifice and obedience?

Here is the point: *ideas have consequences*. What we believe about the world shapes how we live in the world. The following diagram is a "worldview triangle" we have found helpful in grasping the nature and importance of worldviews:

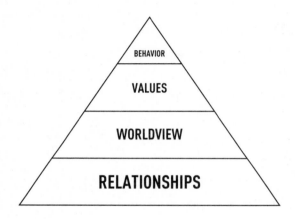

Behaviors are simply the choices that we make. Our behavior is how we act, such as how we treat people, spend money, or use our time.

Values inform our behaviors, which are the things we consider important. A student who values education will work hard at school and save money for college. If you value good health, you will exercise and eat good food.

Worldview determines what we value. For instance, if you hold that people are made in the image of God (worldview), then you will believe they have inherent worth (value) and thus treat them with dignity (behavior).

Our worldview shapes our values, which in turn influences our behavior. And as we explored in the last chapter, worldviews are primarily shaped and learned through *relationships*.

Here are the answers to the above questions about Gen Z:[1]

33% Believe gender is how a person feels, not their birth sex.

49% Believe happiness is defined by financial success.

34% Believe lying is morally wrong.

28% Believe science and church teachings are complementary.

58% Believe many religions can lead to eternal life, as there is no one true religion.

According to Barna research, people who label themselves "Christian" live no differently from those who do not adopt such a label. In other words, there is no net-positive change in someone's behavior for simply identifying as a Christian.

I (J. Warner) will never forget a young man I met named Santiago. I was assigned to a surveillance team

IF YOU'RE A PARENT
MAXIMIZE YOUR MEALTIME

 Parents who regularly share a meal with their children are more likely to pass on their worldview. In one of the central passages of the Old Testament, Moses encourages parents to diligently teach kids at a variety of times, including "when you sit in your house" (Deuteronomy 6:4–7 NASB). Here are a few principles and practical tips for maximizing mealtime:

• Have realistic expectations. Roll with unplanned conversations.

• Don't give up. It can take time to cultivate an environment that values meaningful conversation and interaction.

• Be authentic and don't over-spiritualize everything (Ephesians 6:4). Talking with your kids about things important to them has relational value in its own right.

• Turn off technology so you can be together without distraction.

• Read a passage of Scripture you have personally been studying or reflecting on.

• Discuss a current event.

• Share a prayer request or answered prayer.

• Each person can share a "high" and "low" for the day, or a funny event.

• Talk about a spiritual experience or way God worked in the day. >>

>> • Tell a memory from your child-
hood (or pre-kids) and what you
learned.

• Give a blessing to your kids.
(Recognize positive choices they
make and character traits.)

and had just watched Santiago commit a bank robbery. After arresting him, I transported Santiago to our jail for booking. On the way back to jail, he told me he was *a Christian*. Even he understood the contradiction between the label he embraced and the behavior he exhibited.

Santiago was like many professing Christians who adopt the label but don't live according to the Bible's teachings. However, within the broader segment of people who consider themselves Christians, there *are* some who live *differently*. Who are they? They are those who hold a biblical worldview.

According to David Kinnaman, "People who have a biblical worldview are much more likely to act like Jesus because they see such things as life, people, and crises differently than most people do."[2] In other words, if we want to help young Christians live like Jesus, we need to help them see the world as Jesus did—we need to equip them with a biblical understanding of reality, and help them develop spiritual practices that engrain those beliefs into their lives and character.

Before we look at practical strategies for strengthening the biblical worldview of young people, consider the following four overarching principles:

RECOGNIZE THE COMPARTMENTALIZATION OF FAITH

Today's biggest challenge in teaching worldview to young people is the way our increasingly secular culture fosters the compartmentalization of faith. Our society thinks it is fine to worship on

Sunday at church or to discuss faith in the home, but religious beliefs are supposed to be kept *private*. Our culture rejects the notion that faith should influence how we think about politics, business, or sports—faith is simply considered a matter of personal preference.

This compartmentalization of faith has also seeped into the church. As a Biola University undergrad, I (Sean) remember students packing into the gym for the final chapel of the year. Before worship and the message, a commission was spoken for the students heading to mission trips for the summer. I recall thinking, *Why are we just praying for students going on spiritual mission trips? What about those working as interns at various businesses? Isn't that a mission field too?* Without realizing it, the leaders were encouraging a compartmentalization of the Christian life into the spiritual (mission trip) and secular (job). Yet according to the Christian worldview, *everything* has a spiritual component and the *whole world* is a mission field. We simply cannot separate the two.

This is why we so appreciate the theme at Biola University: "Think Biblically about Everything." In other words, the mission of Biola is to equip students to explore what it means to live out their chosen profession as a Christian. This approach is what every Christian university should be doing. Every church should be making these kinds of connections too. The sad reality, though, is that millions of young Christians have heard their share of Bible-based sermons but have no idea how to live out their faith beyond the walls of the church. A massive fracture exists between their spiritual beliefs and their daily lives. No wonder so many disconnect from the church when it no longer serves their emotional or relational needs.

RECOGNIZE THE CONNECTION BETWEEN FAITH AND KNOWLEDGE

"Christianity is a knowledge tradition." Does that sound strange to you? In the church, we talk about our beliefs more commonly as matters of faith than matters of knowledge. Yet quite interestingly, the word *knowledge* (or a derivate such as *know*) appears more frequently in Scripture than *faith*. Biblically speaking, we are called to trust God with faith. But this faith is not blind—it is based on what we know to be true.

Most people agree that history, math, and science are disciplines that deliver knowledge. And yet Scripture teaches that we can also know things about God. That's right, we have knowledge of God (Proverbs 9:10) just as we have knowledge of events in the past or mathematical theorems. We can know that we have eternal life (1 John 5:13).

Our job is to equip the next generation with knowledge of God. But that is not enough: we must also help young Christians to *know that they know truth*. Let us explain. Our churches are filled with people who know truth, but how many can explain how they know their beliefs are true? Not many. The numbers are even less with Gen Z. This is important because confidence comes not from merely knowing truth, but from *knowing that you know truth*.

Imagine two different students taking a test. Both have knowledge of the material, but one student studies and prepares for the test, while the other doesn't. Which one is more likely to cultivate the right instincts and mark the correct answers during the test? Clearly the one who studies and not only knows truth but also knows that she knows truth.

And here's the key: the one who studied learned the right answers, but she also habitually developed an intuitive sense of the truth and the confidence to respond correctly during the pressure of the exam.

The same is true for our relationship with God. We must help young Christians come to know that they know truth—through both correct information and formative practices—so they can live out their beliefs with clarity, consistency, and conviction.

RECOGNIZE THE DIFFERENCE BETWEEN COMPETING WORLDVIEWS

Endless counterfeits vie for the allegiance of this generation. In the last chapter, we considered relational counterfeits. In this brief section, we

IF YOU'RE A YOUTH PASTOR OR MINISTER
FOCUS ON WORLDVIEW

 In serving as youth pastors, we both have taught biblical worldview through trial and error. Here are some practical ideas we have learned along the way:

• Make regular worldview and apologetics connections in your teaching. Intentionally link biblical truth to your students' lives and relationships.

• Teach a specific unit on worldview. Set aside a predetermined number of weeks to focus on teaching students how to think Christianly (see appendix).

• Lead a weekend retreat with an apologetics or worldview theme.

• Attend an apologetics or worldview conference. We highly recommend sending your students (and joining them) to Summit ministries.[3]

Here are nine teaching strategies we have found helpful:

1. Lecture
2. Discussion
3. Case studies
4. Movies
5. YouTube or other videos
6. Role-playing
7. Guest speaker
8. Visit a religious site
9. Offer an equipping seminar for parents >>

>> Try not to think of worldview as something you do in addition to your normal ministry with students. Rather, see your ministry as always seeking to fortify students with a Christian worldview so they can live out their faith with clarity and boldness as ambassadors for Christ.

are describing worldview counterfeits. Here are three of the more pressing ones for Gen Z:

Naturalism is the belief that God does not exist and natural forces are sufficient to explain everything. This would include worldviews such as secular humanism, Marxism, and existentialism. According to naturalism, there is no God, soul, or other supernatural beings. Naturalism is hugely influential in universities, media, and popular culture. Twice as many Gen Zers identify as atheist compared to the US adult population.[4]

Pantheism is the belief that *all* is god and distinctions are artificial. Pantheistic beliefs can be seen in modern New Age practices such as channeling and astrology. New Age beliefs have been around a long time, but they are being made increasingly palatable for younger generations.[5]

Individualism is the view that life is about *me*. The purpose of life is to be authentic to yourself and to live according to your feelings without obligation to anyone or anything beyond the self. Sin involves being inauthentic, and salvation comes from discovering "yourself." Individualism is particularly alluring to Gen Z because they have been raised with music playlists, newsfeeds, streaming content, and consumer goods being available whenever, wherever, and however they want them. This teaches teens that they are the center of the universe and that reality will tailor itself to their needs.

There are many more worldviews to consider, such as post-modernism, Islam, hedonism, consumerism, pluralism, and so on. With information bombardment, this generation experiences countless belief systems at their fingertips. We must help young people identify false worldviews that compete for both their hearts and their minds (see Colossians 2:8).

RECOGNIZE THE IMPORTANCE OF INTENTIONALITY

One thing we know about equipping youth with a biblical worldview is that it will not happen by accident. Although circumstances vary based on our relationship with students (teacher, youth pastor, parent, mentor, etc.), we each must be thoughtful in our approach.

Bestselling author and Christian leadership expert John Maxwell once wrote, "Nobody finishes well by accident."[6] Results are dependent on our *plan for success*. If we hope to ready students with a Christian worldview, we need to be *intentional*. In chapter 6, we will offer a strategy for training with intentionality, one that will guide your efforts as a parent, youth leader, or Christian teacher.

STEPS FOR EQUIPPING YOUNG CHRISTIANS WITH A BIBLICAL WORLDVIEW

With these four foundational principles in mind, here are a few practical suggestions for equipping this generation with a biblical worldview.

SOMETHING TIMELY

 Many young Christians today have doubts and questions about their faith. Given their exposure to endless viewpoints, it makes sense they would wonder: *Can I really know truth? How can I be confident in my beliefs when other people, who see the world differently, are certain about theirs?*

Questioning is a natural experience for many Gen Zers. But it need not destroy their faith. In fact, doubt itself is not necessarily destructive to faith—*unexpressed* doubt *is*. We need to encourage students to express doubts and ask questions but assure them we still love them and will help them find answers.

SHIFT TO WORLDVIEW THINKING

The first step in equipping this generation is shifting our own thinking about faith. We must refuse to compartmentalize our spiritual beliefs to the religious aspect of our lives. There is a Christian way to think about everything. That's right, *everything*.

Colossians 2:3 says that in Christ are "hidden all the treasures of wisdom and knowledge." Knowledge and wisdom begin by properly understanding God's character and being in relationship with Him. Once we understand the world, and our place in it, we can see that God is ruler over all. As the Dutch philosopher and theologian Abraham Kuyper once said, "There is not a square inch in the whole domain of our human existence over which Christ, who is Sovereign over *all*, does not cry, 'Mine'!"[7]

For example, there is a Christian way to approach health. The Bible teaches that we are both body and soul (Genesis 2:7; Matthew 10:28). Thus, healthy living involves caring for both the body and the soul. We care for the body by getting sleep, eating well, and exercising. And we care for the soul through solitude, confession, and prayer.

There is also a biblical way to approach government. The framers of the United States separated the government into three main branches—legislative, judicial, and executive. Why? One contributing factor was their recognition of the fallen state of humankind. They understood that power corrupts and so they spread it out to minimize the effects of human sinfulness. By contrast, Marxism fails largely because it assumes greed comes from inequality in the distribution of material goods in society rather than the fallenness of the human heart, as Jesus taught (John 2:24–25; Mark 7:21–22).

We must begin to recognize that there is a Christian way to think about *everything*.

GROW YOUR OWN WORLDVIEW

We can pass on to the next generation only what we have first inculcated into our own lives through both *correct thinking* and *right practice*. If we want to help young Christians develop their worldview, an important first step is to build our own. Consider the following practical ways to help you think more deeply about theology, worldview, and apologetics:

- Read a theology, apologetics, or worldview book(s)
- Watch some videos
- Attend a class at church (or start one)
- Attend a conference
- Follow worldview experts and apologists on social media
- Intentionally engage others in conversation on worldview topics
- Listen to a theology, worldview, or apologetics podcast

IF YOU'RE A CHRISTIAN EDUCATOR
FOR YOUR STUDENTS

You have the unique opportunity to directly influence young Christians. You may see some students more than their parents do! If you teach a subject such as math, history, or science, you may feel "time crunched" to get through the required material. But you can do some intentional things in the classroom to develop a Christian worldview:

• Find and share practical ways in which your subject area and the Christian worldview intersect.

• Discuss current events that overlap with your class and the Christian faith.

• Share about influencers in your subject area who were motivated by their Christian faith (e.g., Christian scientists, mathematicians, or historical figures).

• Relate stories from your life or education. Without preaching, personal anecdotes can encourage, motivate, or convict students.

• Show a movie clip or a YouTube video that makes a connection between your subject and faith.

These efforts do not have to take a lot of class time. It could be as simple as five minutes every Friday at the beginning of class. If you plan these intentionally, you might be surprised how memorable they are and how much they influence your students.

• Get formal training through an online certificate program or a graduate degree in apologetics

HELP STUDENTS PRACTICE THEIR FAITH

Equipping students with a biblical worldview is not a matter of mind transformation alone. We all have had the experience of failing to live out something we believe. Why does this happen? The answer is because we are not merely thinking beings.

As James K. A. Smith observed, our wants, desires, and longings are at the core of our identity.[8] In other words, we do not act simply from what we *believe*, but also from what we *love*. This is why we defined a worldview not merely as a set of beliefs, but also as an orientation of the heart. Building a worldview involves learning how to properly love the things of God.

As our friend Jonathan Morrow said, students need the "Three Rs": *reasons, relationships,* and *rhythms.*[9] We can influence these directly—how they think (reasons), who they are with (relationships), and what they practice (rhythms)—and *indirectly* influence what they love and desire as their character is formed. Practices are key to that.

Because love is a virtue that is often learned through practice, by providing young people with experiences, we can help connect their hearts and minds. Consider these options:

- Teach young people the biblical view of poverty, and then take them to serve the poor.
- Whenever you discuss a topic, ask, "So what? How does this affect the way we should live today?" Make practical connections from biblical truth to relationships.
- Explore the biblical view of the unborn, and then take your teens to visit a pregnancy resource center to learn about loving and serving women with unplanned pregnancies.
- Creatively develop certain rituals in your family, church, or school that can help young people cultivate a love for God. This could be a prayer or worship song before class or dinner, a short Bible reading, or the sharing of a story that helps students feel the truth of the lesson.

ENGAGE IN WORLDVIEW CONVERSATIONS

In the last chapter, we encouraged you to have conversations with young people. This is critical because safe dialogue with a trusted

SOMETHING TIMEWORTHY

Which aspect of worldview influence seems most challenging?

_____

_____

_____

How might you meet this challenge and better prepare yourself to communicate the truth to young people?

_____

_____

_____

adult is the best relational medium to learn to think biblically. Because of the ubiquity of information, this generation needs to know _how_ to reason more than to simply learn _what_ to think.

This is best done through asking thoughtful questions (and, of course, being a good listener). We hope you will take seriously the challenge and opportunity of engaging youth in thoughtful conversations. When you do, keep a few things in mind:

- Resist the urge to give easy answers. Students can quickly Google simple responses.
- Ask inquisitive questions that unlock deeper understanding.
- Guide young people to discover truth for themselves.
- Be careful not to come across as judgmental. We are not saying to never show disapproval, but to simply value understanding before being critical.
- Through your body language, words, and actions, be sure young people know you are a safe person to talk to.

Jesus provided His followers with *the* biblical worldview. As the *source* of truth, He understood that His claims affected *every* aspect of reality, and He helped His followers practice what He taught them. He shared meals with the people He met and engaged them in meaningful spiritual conversations. He asked dozens of questions, even though He knew the answers, and led people to truth and to faith. If we want to equip young people with a biblical worldview, we must simply follow His example.

WILL YOU SHOW ME?

PREPARING YOUNG PEOPLE FOR THE FUTURE

Chapter 5

LOVE *IGNITES*
DEVELOPING A PASSION FOR TRUTH

"Ethan, stop arguing with Jim!" shouted John as he sat next to me (J. Warner), preparing the opening statement for perhaps our most publicized homicide trial. Ethan, John's co-prosecutor in the case, was sitting across the table from us. He had abandoned any effort to help John about thirty minutes prior to the outburst. Instead, he was deeply engaged in a conversation with me about the existence of God. Ethan was (and still is) a committed skeptic, passionate about his views and eager to talk with anyone who disagrees with his commitment to atheism.

"Jim loves it when you ask all these questions," continued John. "He'll talk to you about this *all day long*, and if you keep this up, we're never going to get anything done. You need to be more like *me*. Jim knows *I don't care* about any of this God stuff. That's why we don't waste any time talking about it."

SOMETHING TIMELY

It's been widely reported that Gen Z is the least religious generation in history. Just 59 percent of thirteen- to eighteen-year-olds say they are Christian. But that doesn't mean young people aren't interested.

An increasing number of young people simply don't think Christianity is evidentially true. In one poll, nearly half of the teens said, "I need factual evidence to support my beliefs" (46 percent), and Gen Z teens are far more likely to be uneasy with the relationship between science and the Bible (only 25 percent saw the two as complementary).[1]

If we want to increase the passion our young people have for God and Christianity, we'll have to help students see that Christianity is demonstrably (and evidentially) true.

John was right. In the nearly twenty years I have worked with him, he's the least interested person I know. It's been difficult to talk with him about God or Christianity. He's not pretending, either; he truly *doesn't care*, and his apathy has paralyzed our conversations. But John is one of my dearest friends. I love him like a brother, and I can't imagine living in eternity without him.

Maybe you've had a similar experience with someone *you* love. If you're investing in the lives of young people, you've almost certainly experienced the paralysis of apathy. As a youth pastor, I almost always had someone in our group who appeared disinterested. It's difficult to teach the truth to young people you love when they aren't really listening. But that didn't stop me. Because I loved my students, I wanted them to become passionate believers.

Apathy is classically defined as an "absence or suppression of passion, emotion, or excitement" or a "lack of interest in or concern for things that others find moving or exciting."[2] Some of the church's best thinkers now agree that *apathy* may be an even greater challenge to Christianity than *atheism*. In fact, a term has now emerged to describe the growing phenomenon: "apatheism."[3] Journalist Paul

Rowan Brian and writer Ben Sixsmith have argued that "the greatest threat to Christianity is found not in the arguments of the atheist but in the assumptions of the apathetic."[4]

As the growth of the "nones" demonstrates, the challenge isn't in convincing people that God exists or that Christianity is true—it's finding a way to get people to care enough to talk about it. For many, God's existence doesn't seem to matter.

John had no interest in Christianity, even though he was somewhat familiar with its claims. His apathy was rooted in two things: first, he didn't believe there was any evidence for Christianity; and second, he couldn't see why Christianity would matter, *even if it were true*.

Ethan, on the other hand, understood the claims of atheism thoroughly, and he believed his atheistic worldview was supported by the evidence. He was also convinced his view of the world mattered because he thought so much evil had been committed under the banner of religion.

John was apathetic because he didn't think there was any evidence or reason to care. Ethan was passionate because he did think there was evidence and a reason to care.

TWO "WHYS" FOR EVERY "WHAT"

So how can we help young, spiritually dispassionate Christians avoid the apathy of John and the atheistic passion of Ethan? It's not easy, but we think a simple overarching strategy can help ignite a fire like Ethan's and direct it to the truth of Christianity. We call this approach: "Two Whys for Every What."

As pastors, parents, and educators, we've all explained what is true to our young people. *What* do we believe about God? *What* are the claims of Christianity? *What* does the Bible teach about important moral issues? Most of us have engaged these topics at church, home, or school. But simple propositions about the nature of God or the claims of Christianity may or may not ignite a fire in our young people.

That's why we suggest taking two additional steps. For every *what* you offer the young people in your life, be sure to add two *whys*.

First, *why* is the claim you're making true? When teaching about the nature of God, for example, it's tempting to default to "because the Bible says so" when a young person asks us to defend a claim. But take the time to explain the philosophical or evidential support *beyond* the teaching of the Bible. Why is the Bible's definition of God as an eternal, all-powerful, uncreated Creator evidentially reasonable? Why does the Bible's definition of God make sense?

Young people want to know *why* we believe what we believe. If we want them to get excited, we need to help them see that the Christian worldview is reasonable and evidentially true.

Next, help young people understand *why* any of this should matter to them. Once we've described *what* is true and *why* it's supported by the evidence, take the time to explain *why* they should care in the first place. How does this truth impact their lives? How does it change the way they view themselves or the world around them? How does this truth guide or protect them?

This simple approach—two whys for every what—can change the way we preach, teach, or counsel the young people in our lives.

In this chapter, we'll show you how to employ the approach, but first let's examine some simple *passion-building* principles that can set the stage for your interactions:

SEEK GOD

It's important to remember that passion is a matter of the *heart* as much as it is a matter of the *head*. It's an "inside-out" phenomenon, not an "outside-in" manipulation. For that reason, everything must begin with prayer. We've already talked about the role of prayer in connecting with young believers, and it's equally critical when trying to develop their passion. God cares about young believers, and He's eager to empower your efforts. Everything starts in prayer.

Most of us, as Christians, understand the power of prayer and regularly seek God when we are concerned about the people we love. In fact, a recent study found that 61 percent of us pray about the people in our family and community.[5] But I (J. Warner) have something to confess: as a new youth pastor, I seldom prayed about the apathy I sometimes saw in my students. I had been an atheist much longer than I had been a Christian, and I was used to doing things in my own power. So when I first encountered apathetic young people in my youth group, I simply *tried* harder. I would have been far better off *praying* harder.

RECOGNIZE DIVERSITY

As we've described in chapter 2, every young person is different, both in the gifts God has given them and in the way they experience and express passion. This is important to remember when

IF YOU'RE A YOUTH PASTOR OR MINISTER
"TWO WHYS FOR EVERY WHAT" IN YOUR MESSAGES

Imagine preaching through the gospel of John, starting in chapter 1: "In the beginning was the Word, and the Word was with God ..."

Important claims in this verse provide opportunities to answer potential questions:

• Why do we believe Jesus is the Word?

• Why do we believe in one triune God rather than two (or three) different Gods?

• Why should we believe that Jesus is God?

In every message, anticipate and address potential "why" questions as you describe what the Bible says in each verse. Additionally, the next verse in our example describes Jesus as the creator of everything.

• How would this truth change the way your students think of themselves (compared to Darwinian explanations)?

• How might this truth about being designed in the "image of God" elevate their value and identity?

Your students are probably aware of the cultural views related to purpose, identity, and value, given their exposure to the internet. Examine these claims from a biblical perspective. Help your students understand why the claims described in the Bible matter.

you encounter a young person who doesn't seem to be enthusiastic or interested. Some of us are less capable of experiencing passion than others. Just as importantly, some people are simply less expressive, even when they are passionate about something.

We typically assign generalities to people when we haven't taken the time to develop a relationship with them. Before assuming young people are dispassionate, make sure you know them well enough to recognize how they express passion.

MODEL PASSION

Organizations take on the character of their outspoken leaders. Apple, for example, became one of the most innovative companies in the world, largely because its founding CEO, Steve Jobs, was an innovative and passionate visionary. In a similar way, churches take on the character of their lead pastors, classrooms take on the character of their teachers, and families take on the character of their patriarchs and matriarchs.

Our kids know when we're excited about seeing a movie, attending a sporting event, or going to our favorite restaurant. These opportunities are eagerly anticipated and relatively rare. For many of us, however, our experience as Christians is little more than regular church attendance. Perhaps that's why our spiritual lives seem routine and less exciting to our kids. If we can passionately move toward a Christian life of intellectual, emotional, and experiential abundance, our kids just may adopt our excitement. My (J. Warner's) sons still remember the energy they observed around our dinner table when our friends would come over and talk enthusiastically about theology or apologetics. These memories are far clearer than any experience they had at church.

Let your passion for God *overflow* in front of your kids. "The student is not above the teacher, but everyone who is fully trained will be like their teacher" (Luke 6:40 NIV). Become the kind of teacher, leader, or parent your young believers can model.

REMOVE OBSTACLES

It's often said that apologetics can "clear the intellectual obstacles" that prevent people from hearing the gospel. This was certainly the case for me (J. Warner). Once I learned *what* Christianity claimed, I needed to know *why* people thought it was true. My questions, doubts, and concerns fell away, one at a time, as I studied the evidence for Christianity.

In a similar way, there are obstacles that frequently stand between us and the passionate Christians we could become. If left unaddressed, these obstacles can be paralyzing. Here are two we must remove if we want to ignite a passion for God:

Personal Sin

Hidden sin is often the root cause of apathy. It's hard to be passionate about God if you feel like hiding from Him based on the sin in your life. All of us struggle with our sin nature, and young people are no different. As unconfessed sin increases in our lives, so does apathy: "Because lawlessness will be increased, the love of many will grow cold" (Matthew 24:12).

When you encounter apathy, consider the possibility that sin may lie at its core. Examine your own life and encourage the young people you lead to examine theirs as well.

For example, a Barna Group survey commissioned by my (Sean's) father found that 72 percent of young, nonpracticing Christian men between the ages of thirteen and twenty-four view pornography regularly (41 percent for practicing Christian men of the same age group).[6] One study found that 77 percent of young Christian men between the ages of eighteen and thirty view porn at least monthly, and 36 percent look at porn at least daily.[7] Pornography is perhaps the most pervasive hidden sin within the church, and it may not be a coincidence that apathy toward the things of

God is *increasing* at the same time access to pornography is *rising*.

If you want to grow your own passion toward God and the passion of the young people you love, be honest about any hidden sin in your life. Don't allow it to rob you—or your young people—of your and their passion.

Misplaced Priorities

As a youth pastor in Southern California, I (J. Warner) often felt like I was competing with an ever-growing collection of alternative activities. Many of my students missed opportunities to grow and learn as part of our group because their families prioritized club sports or other activities. It's not hard to understand how this might happen, given their value and worth in their own right, combined with the pressure to compete. But if we want to develop a passion for God, we have to rein in the passions that distract us from God. It all comes down to our *priorities*.

I (J. Warner) eventually began to encourage the parents of my students to make their kids' *spiritual formation* a priority, and to do so by rethinking their calendars. We spend time and money on the things we love most. If we want to increase our passion for God (or help others increase their passion), we need to prioritize God. Consider the way you're spending time. Have your misplaced priorities become an obstacle?

IF YOU'RE A PARENT
"TWO WHYS FOR EVERY WHAT" IN FAMILY LIFE

When my (J. Warner's) kids were young, we committed—for a season—to a Sunday night activity. We gathered in the living room around a portable whiteboard with several colored markers. I created a visual board game (modifying similar resources from online). Sometimes it was a word search, crossword puzzle, or match game. I took a little time to craft the activity to teach one "what" and two "whys."

It didn't take long to play the game, but the conversation it started afterward was worth the short effort. We awarded prizes occasionally and made sure our time studying theology and apologetics was every bit as engaging as other group activities we did as a family. We ignited our kids' interest by showing them why the claim was true and helping them see why it mattered.

You don't have to wait for a scheduled family gathering to teach "two whys for every what." When you hear a claim on the radio, in a movie or video, or just around the dinner table, help your kids define the claim (the "what"), ask them if they think there is any evidence to support the claim (the first "why"), then ask them why the issue matters (the second "why").

CULTIVATE RELATIONSHIPS

Your calendar reveals more than just your love of God. It also exposes your priorities related to the people in your life, including the young people you're trying to energize. Deep relationships require time, and lonely Gen Z students are far more likely to embrace our passion if we are willing to devote the time to interact with them in meaningful ways.

We've heard some experts address the problem of apathy by suggesting that youth pastors and teachers should focus more on the young people who are engaged rather than "waste" time on those who are not. Nothing could be further from the truth. If we want young people to care passionately about God, we need to first show that we care passionately about them. If you're witnessing apathy in your young people, it may be time to demonstrate your care for them by giving them more of you.

We've discovered something in our roles as pastors, teachers, and parents: it's easier to stoke enthusiasm in a smaller group than it is in a larger one. We've spoken to groups where thousands of young Christians were assembled, and we've also led small teams of twenty students on mission trips. It's far easier for the apathetic to hide in a large audience than in a small group. We've given successful talks in large settings without ever developing a single relationship, but it's nearly impossible to effectively lead a small group without developing a strong bond.

Relationships are built on time and attention, extended opportunities and small ratios. If you want to transfer a passion for God to the young people in your life, building relationships will serve as the conduit for this energy.

DEFINE TRUTH

There is a direct correlation between our understanding of what is true and our level of passion and interest. Imagine, for example, the following scenario: A youth pastor enters the room on a Sunday morning and invites his students to join him for a one-day mission trip to share the truth with people living downtown. The pastor is trying to motivate his congregation by telling them this "lost" people group has never heard what the young Christians are about to share. But before he piles everyone into the church's van, he tells the group the *truth* he wants them to communicate with the people they meet in the city: their *preference for cookies*.

How many of these young believers do you think would be willing to go on this kind of "mission trip"? How many would take time out of their lives to make a case for their *favorite cookie*? Not many, we suspect. Few people are interested in going out of their way to

SOMETHING TIMELESS

Don't underestimate the power *community* has to extinguish apathy. The earliest believers met regularly and "everyone kept feeling a sense of awe" (Acts 2:43 NASB). Why were they so consistently amazed? What was it about this community that ignited a passion in the earliest believers?

These followers of Jesus "were continually devoting themselves to the apostles' teaching" (verse 42 NASB). When a community reads God's Word, God uses the enthusiasm of more passionate believers to elevate the interest of those who might otherwise be less energized. In addition, when believers share stories of the "many wonders and signs" that take place in their lives (verse 43 NASB), the excitement of God's provision and intervention becomes contagious.

convince someone of a *subjective opinion*.

But what if that same youth pastor wanted to share a different kind of truth with the people living in the city? What if he asked his group to share the cure for tuberculosis (TB) with people who had contracted the disease and didn't even know it was killing them? Unlike a *subjective opinion* related to cookies, this truth would be an *objective claim* about the cure for TB. Do you think the youth group would experience an increased sense of urgency and desire to save those who are dying unaware? We think they would.

That's why it's important to teach young people the difference between *subjective opinions* and *objective truths*, especially for individualistic Gen Z believers. If Christianity is considered to be just a subjective opinion (an individualistic *preference* about God) and not the unique and only cure for spiritual death (regardless of an individual's personal opinion), don't be surprised when young people treat Christianity more like a cookie than a cure. We can teach them what is true, but if we don't first help them understand that Christianity is an objective claim about reality (based on good evidence), they won't understand the urgency—or embrace the passion—that's appropriate for objective truth claims.

One way to increase passion, urgency, and excitement is simply to teach the difference between subjective and objective truth claims and make sure your young people understand that Christianity falls in the second category rather than the first.

RAISE EXPECTATIONS

Theodore Roosevelt once said, "Nothing in the world is worth having or worth doing unless it means effort, pain, difficulty ... I have never in my life envied a human being who led an easy life. I have envied a great many people who led difficult lives and led them well."[8] Challenges add value to everything we do, and we get excited about (and prioritize) the things we perceive as *valuable*. If you want young people to engage God with passion, don't be afraid to challenge them with difficult concepts, thought-provoking ideas, and tough tasks. That means raising the bar and elevating the expectations you have for the young people you lead.

I (J. Warner) can still remember the first time I took a group of students to the University of Berkeley for a six-day mission trip. After witnessing on the campus, engaging with atheists in the Bay Area, and interacting with atheist student groups, I asked each of our students to prepare a message for our group, addressing the objections they encountered over the past several days. I told them that we would video record the presentations and then critique and play them later for our group back home.

I could tell that many of our students were intimidated by the assignment, and it occupied much of their free time over the course of the trip. Each student studied and rehearsed their presentations.

IF YOU'RE A CHRISTIAN EDUCATOR
"TWO WHYS FOR EVERY WHAT" IN YOUR LESSONS

 If you teach in a Christian school setting, you're probably already telling your students about the claims of the Bible ("what" is true) and perhaps providing them with evidence to support these claims ("why" it's true).

If you're still seeing disinterested students, try spending more time talking about why it matters. Provide a second "why" for every "what." Questions to consider:

• How does this truth impact your own identity as a person? Does it help you see your role in the world? Does it change the way you think about your purpose in life?

• How does this truth change the way you see your friends and family? Does it cause you to be more (or less) patient, compassionate, or understanding?

• How does the Christian view differ from alternative views on this topic? Why does the Christian claim do a better job explaining reality than any of the alternatives?

• If we made a list, comparing the Christian claim with its alternatives, what are the strengths and weaknesses of each claim? How does each claim impact our lives and the world around us?

Allow these questions to guide your preparation, and be sure to include the reason why Christianity matters as you teach its principles and doctrines.

The results were impressive, but more important than the content of each message was the confidence that emerged with each messenger. The students felt valued and trusted because we treated them like adults and elevated our expectations for them. And when they met our expectations, we saw their interest and passion grow.

In many Christian youth groups, the emphasis is more on friendship and fun, with a sermonette wedged in between the game, the fellowship, and the pizza. Sadly, young people can play games, hang out, and eat better pizza *somewhere else*. If that's all we are offering—if our expectations are that low—why would we be surprised when our students eventually seek other alternatives? Instead, let's elevate our expectations and allow God's Spirit to ignite a passion.

STAY RELEVANT

Students are typically less interested in school subjects that are difficult to understand or disconnected from their practical experience. Our two "whys" can help us overcome obstacles like perceived disconnects, though. Remember, Gen Z believers are *digital natives* and *researchers*. They have access to the claims of nonbelievers, including their objections to Christianity. If we want our young people to be passionate about the things of God, we need to make sure we show them *why* our claims are true, and *why* they matter in the first place.

Teaching about creation? Make sure you include two "whys" for this important "what." *Why* do we believe in creation? Make the case for intelligent design from biology, physics, and cosmology. Additionally, *why* should anyone care about this question? The claim that human beings are created in the image of God with inestimable worth has several consequences. For example, it would form the foundation for our approach to pornography (we don't look at porn because it uses a person who is meant to be loved). It would also form the foundation for our view of the unborn (we are pro-life because abortion ends the life of a valuable human being). Finally, it would also guide our thinking related to everyday issues like bullying (we oppose bullying because it involves mistreating an image bearer of God). When we provide the *whys* behind the *what*, we open the door for relevance and passion.

DO SOMETHING

Provide young Christians with an opportunity to put truth into *action*. Impatient Gen Z believers will only sit still in an academic setting for so long. Honor their restlessness by creating activities and opportunities that bring claims about God and Christianity to life. We've both seen students become passionate, committed believers after presenting them with options to serve others and share truth.

The apostle Paul knew what he was talking about when he told the believers in Rome to "be devoted to one another in brotherly love; give preference to one another in honor; not lagging behind in diligence, fervent in spirit, serving the Lord" (Romans 12:10–11 NASB). When we serve the Lord, by helping others and sharing the truth, we increase our diligence and fervency. We'll discuss more about this important aspect of passion building in chapter 8.

TAKE A LONG-TERM PERSPECTIVE

Often people who care about students are hard on themselves for "failing" to motivate every student. But here's the reality: *there may be nothing you can do to motivate certain students whose hearts are not open to spiritual things*. Keep in mind, some people even walked away from Jesus in the flesh. Remember the story in which I (Sean) had a student who graduated from my high school Bible class and went on to attend a local junior college. His goal in my class, which he expressed to me, was to get the minimal passing grade (if I remember correctly, he got a C-). And yet, the year after graduation, he came back to sit in my class and encourage other students to pay attention. Why? He was challenged in

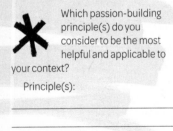

SOMETHING TIMEWORTHY

Which passion-building principle(s) do you consider to be the most helpful and applicable to your context?

Principle(s):

_____

_____

_____

How, specifically, might you employ this principle?

_____

_____

_____

his faith by professors and started taking his beliefs more seriously. When I asked him if I could've done anything differently to motivate him in high school, he said that he wasn't ready spiritually but that he did listen to my lessons probably more than I thought. Even if a student is apathetic, you might be surprised how much he or she is actually learning. Take a long-term perspective and realize that your efforts may not show up for years.

REMEMBER THE "WHYS" WHEN ADDRESSING THE "WHAT"

Sometimes the goal of creating passion in students who seem disinterested can feel like a daunting task. If you change only one thing about the way you've been teaching the Christian worldview to your kids, students, or youth group, let it be this: remember to provide two "whys" for every "what." You will energize young people by helping them see *why* the claims of Christianity are true and *why* these truths *matter*.

Chapter 6

LOVE *TRAINS*

RESISTING THE DESIRE TO ENTERTAIN RATHER THAN TRAIN

"Jim, can Joey and I meet with you?"

I (J. Warner) immediately felt some trepidation about the request. Joey's dad sounded serious over the phone, and I could hear his voice quiver as he described the problem to me. Joey was a member of our youth group before I became the pastor, and during my first year, he was one of the students I worried about most.

He was bright, friendly, and engaging. But he had been hanging out with friends who introduced him to drugs at an early age. Joey was slowly slipping away from our group, from his family, and from his commitment to Jesus.

Joey had been an active member of our group for several years. He was attracted to the activities we hosted, and like many other youth groups in Southern California, our calendar was filled with camps and outings involving board sports of one kind or another. Spring wakeboarding. Summer surf camp. Winter snowboarding. At each of these events, we managed to slip in a Christian message at the end of the day, but if I'm honest, that wasn't our true focus. Far more time was spent *entertaining* our students (and their friends) than *teaching* or *training* them as Christian believers.

Now, after only a year as Joey's pastor, I couldn't help but wonder if our priorities as a youth group were misguided. Could we have changed the trajectory of Joey's life? Maybe. Maybe not. But his situation highlighted an imbalance in our engagement with the students. We were more focused on mirroring the priorities of our culture rather than igniting a passion for God. Joey's story was just another motivation for me to redesign our approach and move from *entertaining* to *training*.

In my first year as the youth pastor, I taught several short series from biblical texts. Eight weeks in Ecclesiastes. Ten weeks from the book of James. I tried to remain true to the text, teaching line by line, and I did my best to faithfully communicate the Word of God. But something was missing. I struggled to define a specific *purpose* for my approach. What was our ultimate goal? The spiritual development of our students? How, precisely, would we know if we were achieving this goal? How could we accurately measure our progress? It dawned on me that teaching is *not* the same as training.

SOMETHING TIMELY

A recent study on Millennials and their critical-thinking skills revealed that even after attending college, they didn't feel confident that they possessed the ability to identify false claims and thought this contributed to the spread of false information on social media.[1] Not much has changed with Gen Zers.

The training model and three-pronged approach we offer in this chapter will help you shift from teaching "what to think" to "how to think" as you assess the claims of Scripture and evaluate how these claims impact our behaviors.

THE DIFFERENCE BETWEEN TEACHING AND TRAINING

Training—to put it simply—is *teaching toward a challenge*. Athletes train in preparation for an athletic contest. First responders train to prepare for the challenges they will face in their next shift. Training is *goal oriented*. The challenge is already on the calendar, and as it approaches, each trainee experiences a sense of urgency and healthy apprehension. The calendared challenge infuses the preparatory teaching with meaning. The teaching suddenly matters, because without it, each trainee will be unable to meet the challenge successfully.

This simple "TRAIN" acronym describes the training process we've used with students:[2]

T – TEST: CHALLENGE YOUR STUDENTS TO EXPOSE THEIR WEAKNESSES

We begin by showing our young people how much they *don't* know by exposing them to the objections of nonbelievers or alternate views from differing religions. One of the very best ways to accomplish this is by inviting someone from one of these differing groups to speak to students about what they believe. If this isn't possible, we've also successfully role-played as an atheist or someone from a different religious system.

R – REQUIRE: EXPECT MORE THAN WE THINK STUDENTS CAN HANDLE

As we discussed in the last chapter, we then raise the expectations we have for each student, offering this elevated expectation as a sign of respect. In other words, we treat them as responsible adults,

IF YOU'RE A PARENT
TAKE ADVANTAGE OF TAB OPPORTUNITIES

The TAB training model, based on theology, apologetics, and behavior, encourages you to initiate conversations with your kids by allowing one of these three categories to act as a catalyst. Here are a few examples:

• When a loved one dies, or something bad happens to a friend or family member, use the opportunity to discuss Christian theology related to the afterlife or to the problem of evil.

• When someone in a movie or on television treats Mohammed, Buddha, or Jesus as if they were just religious leaders, talk about the evidence for Jesus' divinity or the evidence for the resurrection.

• When a friend gets in trouble at school, talk about how behaviors are tied to worldviews and why the Christian worldview can guide and protect us.

In each of these cases, allow the theological, apologetic, or behavioral catalyst to start the conversation, but make sure you include all three categories (and two "whys" for every "what") in your discussion. Make sure your kids connect that our theological foundations can be supported evidentially and ultimately result in behaviors that help us understand our role in the world.

ready and capable to take on the challenges we are going to schedule for them.

A – ARM: TEACH STUDENTS THE TRUTH SO THEY CAN DEFEND IT

Next, we carefully examine the claims of Christianity in light of the common objections offered. This means guiding our students through the written work of skeptics and heretics as well as teaching them the truth from God's Word. This takes time—eight to twelve weeks prior to any challenge we might calendar—and it is specifically targeted at the challenge students are being asked to accept.

I – INVOLVE: DEPLOY STUDENTS INTO THE BATTLEFIELD OF IDEAS

This is perhaps the most important aspect of training: We craft a challenge for our students and set it on our calendar. The entire training process is pointed toward this challenge (more on this in the next chapter). The culminating event is designed to motivate students to attend and participate, and the teaching that occurs in the weeks prior to the calendared challenge takes on a sense of importance and urgency as the date approaches.

N – NURTURE: TEND TO THE WOUNDS STUDENTS MAY SUFFER, AND MODEL THE NATURE OF JESUS

Finally, we prepare for the inevitable "bumps and bruises" students will suffer as they encounter people who oppose Christianity and resist their efforts to share the truth. This could be an unkind word spoken to a young Christian or deep-seated doubts that emerge in discussion with someone from another faith. Regardless, strong relationships are critical to pastorally nurture young people experiencing personal struggles. As leaders, teachers, and parents, we can draw on the "capital" of our relationships *if* we've invested in our young people prior to difficult times. But this will also require us to know the truth well enough (to become the source of knowledge described in chapter 3) to guide our students when they meet a counterfeit.

Every one of us, whether we are parents, youth workers, or Christian educators, must decide what we are going to teach our young people about God and living as a Christian. But more importantly, if we want to energize them beyond the classroom, we need to create reasonable, engaging challenges and then train our young people toward those opportunities.

WHAT IS THE CONTENT OF OUR TRAINING?

As a youth pastor, I (J. Warner) discovered quickly that many of the parents of my students didn't really care what I taught their children, as long as it resulted in "proper Christian" behavior. One honest father once told me, "If your youth group can keep my kids from using drugs and having sex, I would consider it a win!" That rather candid sentiment may be more common than you think. In my first year on the job, many of the topics I engaged with my group were entirely about appropriate behavior. But that obviously didn't stop Joey from slipping into narcotic use.

So what areas of instruction are most important for developing energized, committed young believers who hold a biblical worldview? What broad categories should we explore as we design challenges that turn *teaching* into *training*?

In the last chapter, we introduced a simple "two whys for every what" strategy that will serve us well now as we chart three classes of Christian truth (one "what" and two "whys"). We call this approach "TAB Worldview Training":

THEOLOGY (DOCTRINE)

We begin by describing *what* is true. It's a lot easier to spot a counterfeit once you know what the original looks like. That's the case for Rolex watches, $50 bills, and even claims about God. Our young people need to know what the Bible teaches, especially at a time when most Christians don't.

A recent study found that while nearly 87 percent of American households possess a Bible, most who live in these homes (53 percent) rarely open them.[3] Only 19 percent of Christians say they read the Bible every day, and only 20 percent report thinking about biblical truths throughout the day.[4] Perhaps as a result, only 17 percent of "Christians who consider their faith important and attend church regularly *actually have a biblical worldview*."[5]

Unsurprisingly, a biblical *worldview* is grounded in biblical *teaching*. You can't align your life to the truth of the Bible if you don't even know what it says. That's why everything begins and ends with the study of God as revealed in Scripture: *theology*. The term is derived from two Greek words, *Theos* (Θεός), meaning "God," and *-logia* (-λογία), meaning "utterances, sayings, or oracles." The T in our acronym—theology—obliges us to discuss the nature and role of Scripture; the attributes of God, Jesus, and the Holy Spirit; the definition of salvation; the nature of humans; and the role of the church.

A̲POLOGETICS (DEFENSE)

As we said before, every "what" should be accompanied with two "whys," the first of which is "Why is this true?" For every theological claim we make to our young people, we must answer this critical *why* question.

The ancient discipline of Christian *apologetics* began in the first days following the ascension of Jesus. The term is derived from the Greek word ἀπολογία (*apologia*), which means "speaking in defense." Luke used the word to explain Paul's actions in front of King Agrippa (in Acts 26:2), Paul used it to describe his "defense and confirmation of the gospel" (Philippians 1:7 NASB), and Peter used it to encourage believers "to make a defense to everyone who asks you to give an account for the hope that is in you" (1 Peter 3:15 NASB). If you're like us, you probably cringe at using a word so similar to *apologize* when considering the importance of making a defense. That's why we sometimes refer to this activity as Christian "case making" rather than Christian "apologetics."

When challenged in their faith, young Christians eagerly want to know if Christianity can be *defended*. For this reason, as pastors, teachers, and speakers, we've addressed a broad range of issues and objections to the Christian worldview. Our list may seem a bit overwhelming, but we hope it will help you identify common areas of concern to Gen Z. In the appendix, we've listed specific resources (books, curriculums, conferences, etc.) that will prepare you to engage these topics. Remember, youth influencers don't have to be *experts*. Instead, we need to know just enough to guide young people toward truth. Take small steps toward preparing yourself to address the following areas of inquiry using some of the resources in the appendix:

Issues Related to Truth

Does objective truth exist? Even if it does, can it be known? How is truth defined? Why is any one definition of truth superior to another? How can we be confident in our conclusions given our limited capacity as humans? Can something be true for you but not true for me?

Issues Related to God's Existence

What evidence do we have that God exists? Are there signs in the natural world that point to a supernatural being? Hasn't science disproven miracles? If an all-loving, all-powerful God exists, why is there evil or suffering in the world? Can people be good without God?

Issues Related to the Bible

How do we know that the Bible is true? Why should we trust it if it was written only by men? How can we trust the Gospels when they don't even seem to agree with each other? Doesn't science contradict the teaching of the Bible? Doesn't the Bible contain errors? Why does the Bible condone genocide, slavery, and other bad behaviors? What does it mean to consider the Bible authoritative? How do we best interpret Scripture?

Issues Related to Christianity

What about people who've never heard of Jesus? Isn't it unfair to condemn them? I don't believe I am a sinner, so why do I need a savior? If there's a hell, why would a loving God send people there? Why would God allow people to suffer eternally in hell just because they don't accept Jesus as Savior? If Christianity is true, why are so many Christians hypocrites? What about all the historic atrocities that have been committed by Christians? Why are Christians so uptight and strict about sex?

IF YOU'RE A YOUTH PASTOR OR MINISTER
CREATE SOME SERIES

When I (J. Warner) served as a youth pastor, I charted a scope of curriculums that would allow me to teach all three TAB training elements to my students. I created sermon series (six to eight weeks in length) in each category. Here are some examples:

• **The Sacred Life** – A six-week theology series based on the Apostles' Creed

• **Living Above the Lies** – An eight-week apologetics series based on the eight most common objections to Christianity

• **My Life Lived His Way** – A six-week series based on six common behavioral struggles for teens

You can create similar series by using reliable sources on the internet to research each topic (see appendix). The information you gather will form the basis for your original messages that will be customized to suit the needs of your group.

As you are teaching through one of the three TAB topics, be sure to include two "whys" for every "what," connecting the dots between theology, apologetics, and behavior. >>

Issues Related to Jesus

Isn't it narrow minded to think that Jesus is the only way to God? Isn't Jesus simply a myth crafted from prior dying and rising "saviors" like Mithras, Horus, and Osiris? What evidence do we have to demonstrate Jesus even existed? If He did exist, what evidence do we have to demonstrate the resurrection of Jesus really occurred? What is the evidence Jesus claimed to be God?

Issues Related to Alternative Christian Views

If the Bible is true, why do so many Christian denominations interpret it differently? Why do Christians disagree about important but noncentral issues like the age of the earth, the need for baptism, and the end times? If Christianity is true, why don't all Christians agree on political issues?

Issues Related to Alternative Worldviews

If Christianity is true, why do so many other religions produce good, moral, fulfilled human beings? What about miracle claims in other religions? Why should I believe Christianity is true instead of other historic views of God, like Islam, Mormonism, Buddhism, etc.? What if I were born into another religion?

>> In addition, by keeping the length of each series short (between four to eight weeks), you can repeat the material several times each year (and over the course of four years if you're a high school pastor). Create several series in these three categories, revisiting theological, apologetic, and behavioral claims in new ways so students who enter your ministry over the course of a year have the opportunity to learn the truth.

Issues Related to Ethics

If God loves all people, why would He condemn gay people just because they were born with a different sexual orientation? Is Christianity sexist? Is gender binary? How should Christians approach social media? How should Christians think about life issues, such as abortion, euthanasia, and capital punishment? Should Christians care about the environment? What is a Christian position on racial reconciliation?

BEHAVIOR (DEMEANOR AND DEEDS)

The second "why" we described in the last chapter is: "Why does any of this matter to me?" We must help young people understand how the claims of Christianity impact their lives. As our friend John Stonestreet, the president of Colson Center for Christian Worldview, often says, "Ideas have consequences; bad ideas have *victims*."[6]

The claims of Christianity matter, and we have to help Gen Zers understand this reality: The apostle John once wrote, "Whoever says 'I know him' but does not keep his commandments is a liar, and the truth is not in him, but whoever keeps his word, in him truly the love of God is perfected. By this we may know that we are in him: whoever says he abides in him ought to walk in the same way in which he walked" (1 John 2:4–6). Theology and apologetics are not directionless pursuits. They point us toward holy behaviors and provide us with answers to several questions that matter to young people:

Who Am I?

Young people often define their identity in destructive or unproductive behaviors. Dr. Les Parrott, professor of psychology at Northwest University, identifies five common ways teens establish their identity: (1) through status symbols like clothing, smartphones, or accessories; (2) through forbidden behaviors like smoking, drinking, drugs, and sexual activity; (3) through rebellion against parents and authority figures; (4) through mimicking idols like celebrities and well-known personalities; and (5) through cliques that exclude those who are not like themselves.[7] But these fleeting approaches fail to provide young people with a meaningful identity. Our status and distinctiveness in Christ, on the other hand, provide us with a transcendent, *lasting* identity. "If anyone is in Christ, he is a new creation. The old has passed away; behold, the new has come" (2 Corinthians 5:17).

What Is My Purpose?

Our identity is linked closely to our sense of purpose, and young people want an answer to the question: "Why am I here?" Recent studies reveal that people who can answer this question and have a clear sense of purpose and mission (1) sleep better at night,[8] (2) have better cognitive function,[9] (3) possess a more positive self-image and participate less in destructive behavior,[10] (4) experience beneficial changes in gene expression,[11] and (5) even live longer.[12]

Young people, like many of their older peers, seek to find purpose in work, recreation, and relationships. After futilely trying to find meaning in everything this world had to offer, King Solomon ultimately wrote: "The end of the matter; all has been heard. Fear God and keep his commandments, for this is the whole duty of man" (Ecclesiastes 12:13). The apostle Paul was equally emphatic: "For we are his workmanship, created in Christ Jesus for good works, which God prepared beforehand, that we should walk in them" (Ephesians 2:10). People who believe in God are more likely to report a *higher* sense of purpose in their daily lives.[13]

How Should I Live?

God's Word provides guidance and protection to those who "walk in the same way in which Jesus walked." The high virtues and principles of Christianity—wisdom, justice, self-control, courage, faith, hope, and charity—are still the highest ethical ideals of Western civilization. Scripture helps

IF YOU'RE A CHRISTIAN EDUCATOR
DON'T WAIT

 One of the most important steps for Christian educators to effectively train students is to have a scope and sequence that unfolds logically and naturally. For instance, I (Sean) developed this four-year Bible curriculum for each grade in high school when I was the department chair:

9th: Old Testament Survey

10th: New Testament Survey

11th: Systematic Theology, Cults, and Comparative Religions

12th: Apologetics and Worldview

Keep a couple things in mind: (1) We cover other smaller units within this larger framework (e.g., discovering spiritual gifts and dating). (2) We systematically teach apologetics in 12th grade, but we intentionally address apologetics issues throughout the first three years as they naturally arise in the text (inserting teaching from the TAB categories as well). This approach helps kids see that apologetics is not separate from biblical theology but naturally arises in the study of Scripture.

Given that many Gen Zers encounter skepticism as early as the elementary years, it is vital to teach apologetics and theology early and consistently. Reserving apologetics for senior Bible is often too late. Don't assume your students have an adequate understanding of the Bible or how to defend it. >>

every believer navigate the world in which we live. It guides us toward loving, healthy responses and protects us from dangerous, destructive choices.

TAB Worldview Training provides a template by which parents, youth workers, and teachers can begin to train the next generation. We've just described several specific theological, apologetic, and behavioral categories worthy of our time and attention.

HOW, EXACTLY, SHOULD WE TEACH IT?

Now that we've described the *content* of our training, let's take a brief look at a number of simple training imperatives:

BE PERSISTENT

Don't be afraid to revisit TAB topics and questions repeatedly, especially if you're a youth pastor or Christian educator. As an officer, I (J. Warner) spent nearly twenty-five years training. Very little of this effort involved anything new. Instead, it included scenarios and skill sets that I'd been employing for my entire career and had practiced multiple times until my responses were simply a matter of muscle memory. In a similar way, we can't assume that one spiritual

>> If you are a Christian educator of another subject besides Bible, consider getting a copy of the scope and sequence for your Bible department and tying some of your lessons to it. Making a few connections between your subject and Scripture can help students see how the Bible relates to all areas of life.

discussion, lecture, or sermon will be enough to engrain truth into the minds of our young people. Revisit theological, apologetic, and behavioral topics *repeatedly*.

BE BALANCED

Remember that two "whys" for every "what" requires us to be *balanced* in our conversations and instruction. TAB training rests on three legs, discussed in equal proportion. When our conversations get out of balance and lean too heavily on one of these three legs, they may sound lopsided or preachy. Seek balance as you train up the next generation.

BE HUMBLE

In their zeal, some people who begin to explore and master the evidence for Christianity or God's existence may struggle with humility. As Christian apologists, we've both wrestled with this and consciously strive to remember that being knowledgeable about a topic does not make us superior. In fact, there will always be someone who knows more about a topic than we do. Be sure to express appropriate humility to the young people you are training. They will likely identify this humility as a sign of *transparency*, an attribute Gen Zers admire.

BE PRACTICAL

Because of how deep-seated secularism is in our culture, students often do *not* make natural connections from their beliefs to their behavior. That's why it's important to regularly help them see how theology shapes our actions.

As a youth pastor, I (J. Warner) would occasionally role-play (or ask students to role-play) as someone who was tempting others toward inappropriate, un-Christian behavior. What should we do when tempted? What should we say? How should we respond if we fall into such behavior? Role-playing helps young people prepare for temptations before they occur.

In addition, whenever I (Sean) teach a theological topic to students, I always ask, "Why does this truth matter? How does it relate to our lives? In other words, so what?" Ask this question, and help students draw practical conclusions for their daily lives from theological truths.

BE UNDERSTATED

One important expression of our humility involves the way we make the case for what we believe. If I (J. Warner) have learned one thing in my experiences in criminal trials, it's the danger of overstating the case to a jury. Every case has strengths and weaknesses. Be honest with the young people you train. Don't *overstate* the case for Christianity or God's existence, and don't *understate* the opposition's case either. If you do, you'll only set up your students for even greater challenges when they discover the actual extent of the evidence.

BE PERSONAL AND CONTEXTUAL

Given what we've discussed so far in this chapter, you may be asking yourself, "Is there some form of *existing* curriculum that can help me accomplish this task?" The answer is yes ... and no.

As teachers and youth pastors, we've scoured the internet (and the marketplace) looking for curriculum ideas to help us train young people. We've even created curriculums (see the appendix). But these kinds of courses are designed to be used in brief, controlled settings that may look different from your specific situation. For that reason, we suggest you look for available curriculums, online syllabuses, internet resources (and even the TAB outline we've given you in this chapter) as a *starting point*. Use this material to form and supplement your own material. Become a dedicated student and take the time to modify existing plans and curriculums to meet your specific needs.

SOMETHING TIMELESS

The authors of Scripture repeatedly describe the importance of training. King Solomon wrote we should "train up a child in the way he should go; even when he is old he will not depart from it" (Proverbs 22:6), and Jesus told His disciples that "a pupil is not above his teacher; but everyone, after he has been fully trained, will be like his teacher" (Luke 6:40 NASB).

"Train" in the Old Testament passage is the Hebrew word חָנַךְ (*hanaka*), a word that means to "train up," "make experienced," or to "dedicate." The New Testament term for "train" is the Greek καταρτίσω (*katartizó*), a word that means to "fit together" or "prepare." *Training* involves more than just *teaching*. Training *prepares* young people for future challenges.

BE VISUAL

As we described in chapter 2, Gen Zers are incredibly visual, just like their older Millennial counterparts. That's why we started communicating in a new language many years ago.

I (J. Warner) call this language "Visualish." Rather than compose a message on paper and then try to find images to support my words, I try to think visually from the very start. What word picture or visual sequence would help me explain this concept? What visual metaphor has the power to speak a thousand words on this issue? What object lesson can I use to make the case? Start speaking "Visualish" as you use images, props, and video to communicate your message.

I (Sean) am not an artist like Jim, so being visually creative is not as natural for me. This is why I regularly ask creative students for help in designing slides or finding helpful visuals. They are often more than happy to help.

BE ADVENTUROUS

Training isn't training unless it's preparing us for a real challenge. As you provide two "whys" for every "what," point your training toward something *adventurous*. We've repeatedly seen young people get excited about "out of the box" experiences, especially when these experiences seem difficult, exciting, or stimulating. When we first started calendaring challenges for our young people, some of them said, "Are you crazy? You really want us to do *that*?" Then after thinking about it for a few moments, several responded, "When do we go?" Young people have always been drawn to edgy experiences.

Let's create some that will give them confidence that Christianity is true. More on this in the next chapter.

Training begins with a test, moves through a period of equipping, and then ends with a challenge. If we want young people to "abide in Jesus and walk in the same way in which he walked," we'll need to show them what they don't know, provide them with a well-balanced view of Christianity that encompasses theology, apologetics, and behavioral truths, then give them a chance to demonstrate their proficiency.

SOMETHING TIMEWORTHY

Which theological doctrine(s) do you think your young person(s) needs to understand better?

Which apologetic defense(s) do they most need to master?

_____

_____

_____

Which behavioral demeanors and deeds need the most attention?

_____

_____

_____

Chapter 7

LOVE *EXPLORES*
PROVIDING LIFE-CHANGING ADVENTURES FOR STUDENTS

"Pastor Jim?" asked Daniel as he finished a slice of pizza and watched the college students walk back and forth along Telegraph Avenue. "Do you think we'll ever do another wakeboarding trip?" I (J. Warner) smiled and looked at my good friend Brett Kunkle,[1] who was sitting next to me. He started to laugh.

Years earlier I asked Brett to speak at our high school summer camp, one of many board-sport trips our church took in the early months of my ministry. Brett introduced our group to Christian apologetics during that memorable week, and he helped me recalibrate our youth ministry over the next two years.

"Well," I replied to Daniel, "we could definitely add a wakeboarding trip to our calendar, but it would require us to cancel one of these mission trips ..." I paused. Daniel looked thoughtful. Brett and I waited for his response.

SOMETHING TIMELY

A recent study found that Gen Zers see themselves as "responsible" and "are intimately aware not only of troubles and traumas happening in the lives of family members and friends, but of communities around the world."

This study also found that Gen Zers "want to engage in service that has a tangible and lasting impact on systematic and structural problems."[2]

Young people are willing to engage their world in acts of exploration and service. We simply need to guide their efforts and help activate their faith.

"Never mind then," he said succinctly and then continued eating.

As fun as our board-sport camps had been, they really couldn't compare to the TAB training missions that had become a part of our ethos as a group. Daniel had been part of a twenty-five-student team who had just spent the afternoon on the campus of UC Berkeley. Telegraph Avenue is the main street that leads onto the campus; its lively boutiques and restaurants provided a festive environment for our team. We had been sharing the truth of Christianity with students on the campus, and although our students were much younger than their university counterparts, they were equipped and prepared, exploring their faith as Christians in a way that grew both their knowledge *and* their confidence.

Many of these students would tell stories about these trips for years to come. Most would say they were *transformational*. Our Berkeley mission trip was one of several challenges we calendared to turn *teaching* into *training*. These TAB trips were designed to take advantage of our students' adventurous natures and create an environment where young believers could explore their faith and *thrive*.

And they were more popular than *anything* else we did as a group.

IMAGINING THE CHALLENGE

First responders understand the importance of training. Fire, medical, and law enforcement personnel *train* because they know they will eventually have to *deploy*. In fact, there's no point in training at all if you never plan on deploying![3] TAB training comes to life when you schedule a deployment. This single act (of calendaring a challenge) turns teaching into training.

It doesn't take much to activate what you've been teaching your kids or students. You don't have to take a week-long excursion to give your young people a reason to study and take their Christian faith seriously. The challenge can be much briefer, as long as it (1) raises the bar, (2) requires young people to make the case for truth, and (3) pushes them just beyond their comfort zone. Let the following brief list of suggestions become your starting point. We have included these examples because they engage all three TAB categories, and we've organized them from least involved to most demanding:

SURVEYS AND CONVERSATIONS (ONE AFTERNOON)

Conducting a survey and having a conversation about the topic is perhaps one of the easiest ways to "deploy," as it requires the least amount of preparation. Consider engaging people publicly about their spiritual beliefs by using a simple printed survey (we've provided one in the appendix). Most people are open to answering brief spiritual questions, especially if you begin by saying, "We're conducting a survey about people's spiritual beliefs. Do you have a minute to answer a few questions?" We've done this in a variety of settings, using the survey as a launching pad for conversations. If your youth are just getting started, they can use the survey to simply collect information. As they become better prepared, they can use the questions to trigger deeper conversations about the evidence for Christianity.

EVANGELISM (ONE AFTERNOON)

For most of us, the idea of sharing our faith publicly is scary enough to motivate us to prepare well. In fact, *fear* is probably the one thing that keeps people from evangelizing in the first place. *What if somebody asks a question I can't answer?* We've used public evangelism opportunities to form the basis for several weeks of training related to theological issues (What is the nature of Christian salvation and how can we accurately offer the gospel?), apologetics issues (How will we respond to objections about the Bible, Christianity, or the existence of God?), and behavioral issues (How are we to treat people who believe different things about God? How does our status as Christians affect our public identity?).

TEACHING IN A FAMILY OR CLASS SETTING (ONE AFTERNOON)

One of the best ways to *learn* something is to *teach* it. As youth pastors and teachers, we've asked our students to teach a variety of theological or apologetics topics to their classmates or youth group and calendared the day about a month from the assignment. Without needing to be asked, the student-teachers began researching their topics on their own, if for no other reason than they didn't want to look foolish in front of their peers. Ask your kids to teach during your family devotional, or work with your church's pastoral leadership to arrange an opportunity for your students during a Sunday school session or midweek small group meeting. If you teach high school Bible at a Christian school, have your students teach a theological or apologetics lesson to younger kids at the school.

CREATING A YOUTUBE VIDEO OR BLOG ENTRY (ONE AFTERNOON)

Given that Gen Zers are digital natives, this kind of task may be just the kind of thing that would activate their preparation. Create a YouTube channel or simple blog (there are a number of free blog-hosting sites), and ask your students to answer a simple theological or apologetics question on video or in a written format. The public nature of this request can be a real motivation, and you can decide if it's appropriate to allow comments on the video or written post. Set a due date for going live, then tell your students or children that they can distribute the post to friends or family members on social media.

SERVING IN A NEIGHBORHOOD (ONE AFTERNOON OR FULL DAY)

Service projects help students connect the dots between Christian behavior and evangelism. We've helped elderly people and single parents repair their homes, served disabled neighbors who needed their errands run, and cleaned up local parks and beaches. In every opportunity, our Christian service (behavior) eventually opened a door to a spiritual conversation. "Why are you people so kind?" "What motivates you to help me even though I didn't ask?" "Why are you out here on a hot day?" We've used these scheduled events

IF YOU'RE A PARENT
FIND A WAY TO TAKE A WORLDVIEW MISSION TRIP

As pastors and teachers, we've participated in several worldview mission trips. But what if your youth group or Christian school doesn't understand their value? Here are a few suggestions:

• Do your best to explain the value of these trips to the pastors and Christian educators who lead and teach your students.

• Prepare yourself and offer to role-play as an atheist or non-Christian to demonstrate the need for training to your pastor or teacher. Or find someone who can do it.

• Offer to host training meetings, or help lead, train, or escort the students who participate in the trip.

• Offer to help fund the trip or the study materials needed to prepare leaders and students.

• Consider partnering with a group of like-minded parents to take a trip. The principles and guidelines we offer in this chapter will help you lead your own trip.

Pastors and Christian educators have a tremendous responsibility. Be patient and understanding as you try to help them understand the value of a worldview mission trip.

to motivate our students to live out the truth they believe. Often these outings provide the opportunity to ensure that our students know how to both share and defend their faith.

VISITING A LOCAL UNIVERSITY CAMPUS (ONE AFTERNOON OR FULL DAY)

Pick a local university and ask to visit the campus during an academic session so students will be present in the courtyards and common spaces. You can decide whether your students should use the spiritual survey we've described or if they're ready to engage in more traditional forms of evangelism. If possible, arrange a meeting with a student group (either Christian, religious, or atheist) to talk about spiritual matters, or simply ask what life on the campus is like, given their worldview.

SPENDING TIME AT A RELIGIOUS COMMUNITY OR FACILITY (ONE AFTERNOON OR FULL DAY)

We've visited mosques, Mormon wards, Universalist churches, and a variety of religious groups to attend services, ask questions, and engage in conversations. While these trips may seem entirely theological or apologetics in nature, they aren't. Students who attend these opportunities are challenged to learn how to respond in love, even when someone makes a false claim about Christianity. Exhibiting solid behavioral training prior to these trips is crucial.

SERVING AT A LOCAL MISSION OR MINISTRY (ONE DAY)

Our groups have served at local rescue missions, soup kitchens, and churches (like those on Skid Row in Los Angeles). These trips allow us to explore the behavioral commands of Scripture (related to the dignity of every human being, the purpose of our existence, the necessity of serving the poor and homeless), but they also require some theological and apologetics training. Our students almost always engage people with the gospel and find themselves answering questions and objections.

TAKING A TAB TRIP (THREE TO SEVEN DAYS)

The TAB trip is the "granddaddy" of deployments, and although we've saved it for last, we encourage *everyone* to partake in such an event. These deployments occur over several days and nights and are more intensive than anything else we've described so far, but that's what makes them so *transformational*. We've taken several trips of this nature in the following TAB categories:

Theological TAB Trips

Theological TAB trips involve three to seven days at a location in your region that has a high concentration of believers from a religion *other* than Christianity. We've taken our students to Salt Lake City to engage Mormon believers, and to areas in Los Angeles County that have high Muslim populations. Our youth trained for eight to ten weeks prior to the trip, stayed at a local Christian church during their time away from home, and interacted with believers on the street, at the temple or mosque, at local religious universities, and door to door in neighborhoods. To prepare for this trip, students studied the reliability of the Bible, Christian theology, and the claims of the other religion to become the best *Christian theologians* they could be.

Apologetics TAB Trips

Apologetics TAB trips require three to seven days on a secular university campus in your region. We chose the University of California at Berkeley, an aggressively secular campus. Our youth trained for eight to ten weeks prior to the trip, stayed at a local Christian church during their time away from home, and interacted with atheist professors, speakers, and student groups. To prepare for this trip, students studied the evidence for God's existence, the reliability of the Bible, the truth of the Christian worldview, and the philosophical, theological, and scientific objections of atheists to become the best *Christian case makers* they could be.

Behavioral TAB Trips

Behavioral TAB trips involve one to two days helping in ministries that serve the poor, homeless, needy, and addicted. We decided to partner with local ministries for our behavioral trips because we wanted our youth to develop relationships they could continue long after the trip was over. We also wanted them to understand that these issues are local and affect our communities and neighborhoods. We teamed with rescue missions and churches working in the most impoverished parts of Los Angeles County. Our youth trained for three to four weeks prior to the trip, returned home at the end of each day, and interacted with people from a variety of backgrounds. To prepare for this trip, students studied the behavioral commands of Scripture and the biblical definitions of human identity and social justice (a subject Gen Zers are particularly interested in) to become the best *Christian ambassadors* they could be.

While all these activities are useful in creating the kind of deployment opportunities that transform teaching into training, the three- to seven-day TAB trips are *by far* the most effective. For that reason, we'll spend the rest of this chapter trying to help you make these kinds of trips a real possibility for your family, youth group, or class.

SETTING THE CHALLENGE

Begin by establishing the kind of trip you want to lead (related to your efforts to teach theology, apologetics, or behavior). Then determine the date and location for your trip:

PICK A LOCATION

Do some research to see if there is a university, religious community, or service ministry that matches your needs and is within driving distance of your home, church, or school. We've learned from experience that these TAB trips are far more appealing and impactful to adventurous Gen Zers if students are displaced. In other words, do your best to pick a location that is too far for anyone to return home at the end of the day. When we first began planning our *theological* mission trip with Brett Kunkle, we realized that the epicenter of Mormonism—Salt Lake City—was just twelve hours away by car. This provided us with a perfect "high density" location to engage people who hold very different theological views that was also far enough away to provide students with an "unfamiliar" experience.

FIND A FEW PARTNERS

Next, start exploring potential partners to help you host and train your students. You'll need a location that provides sleeping quarters, a kitchen, and a place to meet as a group. For this reason, hotels are usually not a great option. Instead, look for a local church (with a gymnasium, classrooms or youth rooms, and a kitchen). Some churches are willing to donate their facility to a mission team, while others may charge a modest fee. Camaraderie is achieved and relationships are built when students participate in the mission *together*—sleeping, eating, studying, and playing as part of a close community. Church facilities encourage this kind of engagement. In addition, students must learn to work together to maintain and preserve the facility as they exercise Christian behavior and responsibility.

In addition to *housing* partners, look for *training* partners. Use the internet to find experts who live near your mission field. When leading trips to Salt Lake City, we partnered with three excellent Christian apologists who minister to Mormons: Sandra Tanner from Utah Lighthouse Ministry,[4] and Bill McKeever and Eric Johnson from Mormon Research Ministry.[5] When we first started leading trips to Berkeley, we brought our students to visit with Phillip Johnson, the retired UC Berkeley law professor who is considered to be the "father" of the Intelligent Design movement. Excellent teachers,

IF YOU'RE A CHRISTIAN EDUCATOR
GET SOME HELP

 If you would like to add a TAB trip to your calendar but are concerned about the logistics involved, we have a few suggestions:

• First, rather than adding another mission trip to your schedule, examine your school calendar to see if there is something you could replace with a TAB trip—if only for a year on a trial basis. See if your leadership is willing to use the resources and volunteers they would typically use for another mission trip for a TAB trip.

• Second, delegate. When we first started taking these trips, we both knew we didn't have the time or the expertise to succeed on our own. That's why we started by partnering with Brett Kunkle at MavenTruth.com. He's developed a system that will help you get started and eventually equip you to lead trips on your own. Don't carry the load alone, at least at first. Find a champion on your campus, such as a Bible teacher or chaplain, and connect him or her with Brett.

• Finally, start small with a local three-day trip, and work your way up to a five-day trip in another region. It's easier to correct mistakes when you're close to home.

Do what it takes to shift your efforts toward a more comprehensive approach that culminates in a learning adventure your students will never forget.

missionaries, and apologists such as these trained our students while they were on the trip.

LINE UP YOUR OPPORTUNITIES

Every destination also provides its own unique opportunities to engage people who hold different worldviews. Use the internet to find the best local experts representing the group with whom you are interacting. When in Berkeley, for example, we contacted the local atheist association and arranged for three of their speakers to address our group. We also contacted student atheist groups and arranged meetings at UC Berkeley.

In addition to experts, some locations host local events that can be incorporated into your trip. On our trip to Utah, for example, we took advantage of the ongoing summer session at Brigham Young University and the annual Mormon Miracle Pageant in Manti, Utah. This allowed us to engage students on the campus of BYU and participate in street witnessing during the pageant.

In Berkeley one year, we were able to include a local pre-scheduled speech given by Eugenie Scott (the former executive director of the National Center for Science Education) on the topic of creationism and education. Look at the local calendar for your location to see if you can include an upcoming event on your trip.

BUILD YOUR TEAM

Longer TAB trips require a dedicated volunteer team. If possible, include one adult for every four to five students. The majority of these adult leaders should attend all the training sessions for the trip, because you'll need them to help answer questions and counsel students. Remember, however, that responsibilities help create "buy-in" and ownership. Adult leaders should *not* be doing all the work. Instead, these leaders should delegate many of the duties to students:

Driving Team

The number of drivers will depend, of course, on the number of students you are taking. Each driver is responsible for tracking and retaining all the receipts for fuel and the maintenance of each vehicle. If you have a big enough group, you might even consider getting a bus. If this is the case, your driving team will be responsible for the boarding and unboarding of students to make sure everyone is accounted for.

Meal Teams

Separate teams should be formed to plan and prepare breakfast, lunch, and dinner. These adult leaders will (1) select the students they need to help with the meal, (2) make a list of food items and paper supplies that will be needed, (3) coordinate their list with the other meal teams, and (4) purchase all groceries. Be sure to check for any allergies when meal planning.

Worship Team

An adult leader will be responsible for musical equipment and will coordinate students to help lead a time of worship and devotion.

Facility Team

One or more adults will select students to help organize and maintain the proper care of the church you're using to train, sleep, and eat.

Equipment Team

One team is responsible for collecting the equipment necessary for a successful trip, including (1) sports equipment (basketballs, Frisbees, footballs) and games (board games, chess, checkers, playing cards) for free time, (2) sleeping equipment (if needed), like fans and extra sleeping bags, and (3) first-aid kits.

Memory Team

The memory team is responsible for chronicling the trip with images or video. Adult(s) should be assigned to this task, so students are free to engage the mission without distraction.

SET A DATE

Because I (J. Warner) was TAB training with my youth group, I designed our yearly calendar around the TAB trips we've described in this chapter. I took a theological trip to Utah each year in the summer (as soon as school let out in June), an apologetics trip to Berkeley during the winter break (typically around Presidents' Day in February), and two or three behavioral trips (because they are so much shorter) throughout the rest of the year.

As a high school Bible teacher, I (Sean) led either an apologetics, theological, or behavioral trip each year. I wanted every student to be able to take each trip at least *once* (students would miss between three and five days of school). I would also encourage my students to go on an additional trip with their local church.

As you consider setting the date for one of these trips, think about the events you might want to engage in the city you'll be visiting. Also, contemplate how you can weave these trips into your teaching calendar, remembering that every trip is preceded by weeks of training. Make sure to leave yourself enough time to make the most of these training opportunities.

Because you want your students to take these trips seriously (and because there are costs associated), require students to sign up *prior* to the beginning of training. Calculate a cost and tell students—in advance—that you expect them to raise support as missionaries. This will help them understand the nature and purpose of the trip, and it will give them time to defer costs.

PREPARING FOR THE CHALLENGE

Once the training begins, tell students you want to *raise the bar*. Start by role-playing as an atheist or someone from a different religious or belief system. Push your students in order to reveal

SOMETHING TIMELESS

The apostle Paul told his readers: "See to it that no one takes you captive by philosophy and empty deceit, according to human tradition, according to the elemental spirits of the world, and not according to Christ" (Colossians 2:8).

Paul wasn't warning his readers to reject *all* philosophy, but instead to discern the difference between philosophies that were based on human traditions (according to the elemental spirits of the world) and those that emanated from the mind of God.

If we want our young people to be discerning in this way, we need to expose them to errant philosophical and religious claims, help them engage the people who hold these claims, and teach them how to love these people as Jesus commanded.

their weaknesses in answering simple objections or refuting alternate claims. You could consider bringing in a guest speaker to do this, watch and debrief an atheist presentation together, or show them my (Sean's) "Atheist Encounter" video on YouTube. The idea is for them to discover, in a safe environment, how unprepared they actually are to respond to challenges to their faith. Once you've done this, reveal your plan to help them become better case makers by taking them on an adventure unlike anything they've ever experienced before.

Next, pick and assign a reading text. For our Berkeley trip, we used *I Don't Have Enough Faith to Be an Atheist* by Norman Geisler and Frank Turek. Using the chapter structure of this book as an outline, we established a training schedule and required students to be present for at least six of the eight training sessions if they wanted to go on the trip. All the finances for the trip were collected one week *prior* to the training. Parents and students were told that a legitimate excuse was required to miss a training session and that a *third* missed session would result in the student being dropped from the trip without a refund. That may sound harsh, but it energized our training (and not a single student ever missed enough sessions to be dropped from a trip).

Training sessions can take place during your weekly meeting if you're a youth pastor, during your class time if you're an educator, or once a week during your family devotional. Because not all my students would go on the trips, I (Sean) found the best training times were Sunday nights and during weekly lunch meetings. There is a great value in training your entire group or class, even if only a fraction of them have signed up for the trip. We required those who *were* going on the trip to take two written tests in week four and week eight to make sure they were reading the text. We also used the internet to bolster our research material, including videos from prominent apologists that helped make the material visual (see the appendix for suggestions).

ENGAGING THE CHALLENGE

Your mission trip starts the minute you are on the road. While every trip is different, keep in mind these basic principles during your adventure:

REMEMBER TO PRAY

Cover each day—all the people with whom you'll intersect and the important activities within each day—in *prayer*. Model prayer for your team and ask students to take the lead.

IF YOU'RE A YOUTH PASTOR OR MINISTER
TAKE "BABY STEPS"

A TAB trip is probably a new idea for most youth pastors. When I (J. Warner) first started creating a trip for our youth group, I knew our church leadership would be anxious, given the organizational requirements and "risk" of uncharted territory. After all, no one in our church had ever done anything like this before.

For this reason, start small, using some of the suggestions we've offered in this chapter. Consider forming and taking trips in the following order:

- Take your students for an afternoon conducting spiritual surveys at a local shopping center.

- Arrange a visit at a local university for a day to conduct surveys and meet with a student group to talk about issues of faith.

- Arrange a visit at a local Mormon ward, Muslim mosque, or other religious facility to take a tour and engage leaders with questions.

As you take these shorter trips, start talking to your parents and adult leaders about taking a longer TAB trip. Use these shorter excursions to train your adults, to acclimate them to the purpose and benefits of the trips, and to build a team that will support your proposal to church leadership.

Use shorter TAB excursions to pave the way for longer trips and experiences.

TRAIN ALONG THE WAY

Use every spare minute to continue your training. We scheduled training sessions into each trip, and we even selected theological or apologetics CDs and podcasts for the drive.

SET BOUNDARIES

Restrict phone usage. We didn't allow students to bring cell phones; parents had the numbers for the adult team in case they wanted to call, and we posted updates daily. If this seems too strict, consider restricting phone use to fifteen minutes a day, after dinner. In addition, limit students' use of the internet to studying topics related to the trip. (Mission trips like these are Netflix- and Hulu-free environments.) Finally, if a couple in your group is dating, tell them that there will be no outward expression of this relationship during the trip. We want students to be focused on the mission, not on any special relationships. In fact, to promote team building and reduce the amplification of cliques within the group, we required students to perform a "car shuffle" at each stop so students would sit with different members of the group through-out the trip and get to know more people.

MODEL CHRIST

Model Christ always, especially during moments of disagreement. You will likely encounter some people who are aggressive or mean spirited. Respond as Christ would, and model this behavior for stu-dents. Encourage them to ask questions and interact with others "with gentleness and respect" (1 Peter 3:15), even if their efforts are rebuffed, ignored, or criticized. This response may even need to be applied during clashes between fellow team members.

INCLUDE SOME FUN

Students who take these trips usually report that even the most challenging aspects of the trips are *fun*, but we also want to provide them with some "downtime." We schedule free time at the end of every day, allowing students to play games, visit, or just relax. If time permits, we take advantage of local, recreational areas. While in Utah, for example, we spent part of one day hiking to Donut Falls. While in Berkeley, we spent part of a day traveling to Fisherman's Wharf in San Francisco.

DOCUMENT THE TRIP

Be sure to take pictures or video along the way to memorialize how God used your team.

SOMETHING TIMEWORTHY

Which form(s) of training "adventure" seems most feasible, given your context?

_____

Pick one of these possibilities. Plan the following:

Type:

_____

Possible location:

_____

Reasonable time frame to complete the adventure, from:

_____

to:

_____

DEBRIEF OFTEN

Stop to organize your thoughts as a group, answer questions, and respond to issues raised by your guests, speakers, or student activities. Make sure you do this repeatedly, so students can have their questions addressed while they are still fresh in their minds (this is something you should also do if you are taking one of the shorter excursions we described earlier in the chapter). Be sure to ask:

"Did they (the speakers, religious leaders, students, or laypeople they contacted) raise any issues that you felt were troubling, or did they pose a question you couldn't answer?"

"Were you able to spot any logical inconsistencies in their statements or arguments?"

"How does their worldview differ in answering the three big worldview questions?"

"How well were you able to maintain your Christian character while interacting with them? What could you have done better?"

"What do you think you should study (or improve on) so you can do a better job next time you are interacting with people who hold differing points of view?"

CELEBRATE AFTERWARD

Once you return from your trip, schedule an opportunity to share what you experienced with others. If you took the trip as a family, consider hosting a dinner with your friends and other family members. If you're a youth group, ask for a few minutes during the adult worship. If you're a teacher, ask to feature the trip at the next school assembly. TAB trips are impactful. Be sure to share the memories so others can be energized.

As we describe these TAB trips to parents, youth pastors, and Christian educators, most of them eventually ask, "Can you just show us what one *looks* like?" For that reason, we've included two sample schedules from our Berkeley and Utah TAB trips in the appendix.

Young people like Daniel would rather engage their faith actively than surf, wakeboard, or skate. Here in Southern California, that's saying something. Gen Zers are willing to explore their faith in adventurous ways, if only we are willing to prepare them, guide them to the mission, and release their energy.

Chapter 8

LOVE *ENGAGES*

PREPARING STUDENTS THROUGH MOVIES, MUSIC, SOCIAL MEDIA, AND CURRENT EVENTS

In high school, my parents took me (Sean), my older sister, and my girlfriend to see the Holocaust movie *Schindler's List*. You might be thinking, *That's crazy. Why would your parents take you to see an R-rated movie with sexuality and graphic violence?* The answer is because my parents saw it as an opportunity to help me think deeply about the historical and philosophical issues raised by the film. When the movie was done, we discussed it for two hours over dinner. To this day, I still remember much of our conversation.

My parents were modeling an important point: *love teaches kids to thoughtfully and confidently engage the world around them.* When I was in high school in the early '90s, cultural messages came primarily through movies, television, and music. These mediums are still powerful today, but since Gen Zers are the first truly digital generation, we must also teach them how to thoughtfully engage the world of smartphones and social media.

TECHNOLOGY IS AN OPPORTUNITY

My (Sean's) son didn't get a smartphone until he was fourteen and a half. My (J. Warner's) daughters didn't get phones until their junior and senior years in high school. Why so late, by cultural standards? The first reason is that we wanted to protect them from potential dangers to their emotional, relational, and psychological health. As Jean M. Twenge has documented, there is a statistically significant link between smartphone usage and depression, loneliness, and anxiety among Gen Z.[1] Honestly, do kids *really* need one earlier?

But secondly, and more importantly, we saw it as an opportunity to help them learn certain life lessons about responsibility and delayed gratification *before* they got a phone. If you give your son or daughter a phone, or access to social media, too early, you miss a critical opportunity to help prepare them for adulthood.

This is how my (Sean's) parents approached my desire to drive. They never promised I could get my license on my sixteenth birthday. I had to show both maturity *and* responsibility. Otherwise, they were not going to let me get behind the wheel while living under their roof.

And this is *exactly* how we see smartphones. If we give our kids a phone too early, or promise them one at a certain age, we lose the ability to motivate them toward responsibility and character. How will they understand the power of a phone if we don't require them to demonstrate a certain level of maturity before getting one? And if we don't teach them how to use it properly, how can we expect them not to abuse it?

In order to help young people understand the way media impacts the way we think, we must (1) protect them from *negative* media messages, and (2) use media as an opportunity to help kids develop a Christian worldview. Both approaches are vital. Let's start with the first.

RECOGNIZE HOW MODERN MEDIA SHAPES WORLDVIEW

It is no secret that various forms of media shape how young people see the world. As we saw in chapter 4, media messages shape their worldview, which influences their values and, in turn, translates to their behavior. Some argue that media does not affect how people behave. But then why would companies pay millions of dollars for Super Bowl ads? Marketing research shows that what we see translates into how we act.

IF YOU'RE A YOUTH PASTOR OR MINISTER
USE MOVIES TO TEACH A BIBLICAL WORLDVIEW

First, use movie clips in your teaching. Biblical themes are regularly found in movies, if you are willing to look for them. For instance, if you are teaching in James 3:1–12, consider using a clip from the movie *Ant-Man*. James emphasizes that although the tongue is small, it has great power. This is the theme of *Ant-Man*, which can be illustrated by showing a number of different short scenes from the film (available on YouTube). Why not discuss James, show a short clip from the movie, and intentionally make the connection from the movie to the passage?

Second, preach a series through film. There are many online articles and books that offer theological and worldview analyses of various films. Get creative with your approach, just as I (J. Warner) once did with a teaching series based on *The Matrix*. You could analyze some recent movies or you could arrange the series around certain theological or apologetics questions. Find a creative approach and stick with it. To save time, you can show film clips instead of an entire movie.

Third, lead a regular movie group at your home. Serve food, watch different movies, and then discuss each film afterward. Read some articles ahead of time so you're prepared to ask good questions. This is a relational way to help students investigate truth.

Yet it is not only the messages themselves that influence young people. In her book *The Happiness Effect*, Donna Freitas argues that social media creates an incessant *comparison game*.[2] People share the best of themselves online. Young people see the fun other people are having, and when they consider their own comparatively "inferior" lives, it robs them of their joy. The pressure to appear perfect online is one major contributor to why Gen Zers are increasingly lonely, anxious, and depressed. Media shapes not only how this generation *thinks* but also how they *feel*. Media shapes their beliefs, and it also shapes the orientation of their hearts.

ENGAGE KIDS EARLY

In 2012, only half of teens had a cell phone. Today it is around 90 percent. Even if your kids do not have one, *your kids' friends do*. It is simply impossible to shield kids from the temptations and pressures of a world in which many children have unregulated access to everything within one click or tap.

The kinds of pressures kids face, the questions they are asking, and the scenarios they have to confront are historically unprecedented. Take, for example, the access young people have to pornography. It's easily accessible, free to view anonymously, and even socially acceptable. Most parents, youth leaders, and teachers are unsure how to address the world their kids and students view online every day.

Here is a principle we hope you will adopt: *start the conversation with your kids before they are confronted with the issues elsewhere.*

We need to inoculate them with a biblical perspective *before* they are confronted with unbiblical ideas elsewhere. It is a shame that we have to do this. As parents, it breaks both our hearts. But we must realistically and appropriately guide our kids in a broken culture.

MODEL HEALTHY TECHNOLOGY USE

In Deuteronomy 6:4–9, Moses instructed the Hebrew people in how to pass on their faith to the next generation. But before he described guidelines for engaging the young, he first offered two directives to the leaders: "Hear, O Israel: The LORD our God, the LORD is one. You shall love the LORD your God with all your heart and with all your soul and with all your might" (6:4–5).

In other words, Moses instructed the Israelites to *first* make God the Lord of their lives and *second* to love God with everything. Put another way, they needed to first look at their own lives before they started critiquing the next generation. This is good advice to apply to the proper use of technology. Before we criticize the young, we must take an honest look at our own habits. Ask yourself: Do I constantly check social media? Do I feel the need to respond to every

SOMETHING TIMELESS

"Fathers, do not provoke your children to anger, but bring them up in the discipline and instruction of the Lord" (Ephesians 6:4).

In this chapter, we encourage you to be an influencer of young people who seizes opportunities to help them engage culture effectively.

As Deuteronomy 6:4–7 emphasizes, we are to strategically and intentionally instruct young people in the way of the Lord. But there is an important balance we want to stress: be careful not to exasperate the young. In other words, be careful not to overdo spiritual instruction. Finding a balance can be tricky, but the deeper you build relationships with youth, the more likely they will be to heed your instruction and not be provoked to annoyance. Young people need both truth and relationships.

text immediately? Do I have my phone out during meals? Do I post inappropriate material? Parents, do you sleep with (or near) your phone? Do you text while you drive? Can you spend stress-free time away from your phone?

We could ask many more questions. But you get the point: *if we want young people to have good social media habits, it begins with us modeling what that behavior should look like.*

SET HEALTHY BOUNDARIES WITH KIDS

Many of us, as parents, don't want to fight the battles necessary to set healthy boundaries. It is easier to give kids a smartphone, for example, than deal with the complaining and incessant comparisons to other parents. But it misses an opportunity to set healthy boundaries and expectations for our young people.

As kids get older, they should earn more privileges. The goal is to prepare them to make wise decisions when they are no longer under our authority. If kids are given privileges before they have demonstrated sufficient responsibility, they will not value them and may abuse them.

My wife and I (Sean) have allowed our son to get Instagram. But it is only after he has shown that he can handle it (we have his passcode) that we will consider Snapchat. Before getting a phone, our son also read the book *The Teen's Guide to Social Media and Mobile Devices* by our friend Jonathan McKee. He had to agree to and sign a phone contract as well. Here's the bottom line: *setting healthy boundaries communicates to kids that we love them enough to protect them and to help guide them to adulthood.*[3]

For the first part of this chapter, we have discussed ways to *protect* our kids. For the second part, we want to discuss active ways to use media as an opportunity to teach kids how to engage the world as Christians.

WORLDVIEW AS A NARRATIVE

In chapter 4, we defined *worldview* as a view of the world that answers three critical questions: (1) How did we get here?—*Origin*; (2) Why is everything so messed up?—*Predicament*; and (3) How can we fix it?—*Resolution*. In other words, a worldview is a *story about reality* with three components: origin, predicament, and resolution.

We also briefly described the Christian worldview in chapter 4. Other worldviews present a story of reality as well. *Naturalism* says the world is a cosmic accident (origin), humans have messed things up (predicament), and we must solve our own problems (resolution). Naturalism is often portrayed in YouTube videos, memes, songs, and other forms of modern media. In terms of movies, naturalism can be seen in films such as *Sherlock Holmes* (2009), in which scientific analysis is used to explain away every supernatural phenomenon, including an apparent resurrection.

Pantheism says humans are eternally part of the divine (origin), but that we forgot our godhood (predicament), and need to be reminded so we can become one with the universe (resolution). In terms of film, the pantheistic worldview is portrayed throughout the Star Wars franchise as well as in movies like *Moana* and *Avatar*.

Not all movies have a theme that nicely fits into the box of a particular worldview, though. Some promote consumerism. Others emphasize individualism. Some highlight the power of forgiveness. Science fiction films wrestle with questions of human value, free will, and responsibility. Horror movies often raise questions about justice. Comedies often grapple with issues of happiness, the nature of relationships, and the meaning of life. But all movies tell a story about how people should or should *not* live.

Several years ago, when *The Matrix* movie hit the big screens, it quickly became one of the most popular (and talked about) movies among seminarians. I (J. Warner) was in seminary at the time, and my conversations with fellow seminarians soon became the foundation for my own work as a youth pastor. It wasn't long before I was using the movie in my youth group to teach worldview. Why? Because, like other movies, it told a story using the three components of world-view we've already described:

> **Act 1:** *Origin*. This is the introduction to the movie in which we learn about who the characters are and where they are from.
> **Act 2:** *Predicament*. The story unfolds, and something goes wrong. The problem of the story emerges.
> **Act 3:** *Resolution*. The problem is overcome, and we learn what consequences follow for the choices.

This same three-act approach is true for television shows, commercials, YouTube videos, social media postings, songs, and even many video games as well. Consider an emblematic commercial.

A mom is driving her kids to a sporting event. This *origin* reveals that she is a "soccer mom" in the typical middle-class American family. Then something happens, such as another car swerves in front and the kids are put in a *predicament*. Fortunately, they swiftly turn out of the way just in time, because they bought the right tires (*resolution*). Commercials do not merely contain facts about a product but are stories with emotional appeal about how a product both enhances the lives of users and protects them from harm.

MOMENTARY SACRIFICING

Before we offer some practical approaches, let us encourage you to make it a priority to engage with modern media with young people. Have discernment, of course, but be willing to watch YouTube videos, television shows, movies, play video games, and listen to the kinds of music they enjoy. Try to avoid getting overly defensive or

IF YOU'RE A CHRISTIAN EDUCATOR
INCORPORATE MODERN MEDIA

If you teach Bible at a Christian school, try teaching a worldview unit that includes basic principles of critically approaching film and then watching various movies with students and discussing them. To learn how to approach films through the lens of worldview analysis, we recommend reading *Hollywood Worldviews* by Brian Godawa.

I (Sean) have done this for years with high school students. The students and I both enjoy it. They also remember it. Students often say, "I can't watch a movie anymore without thinking about the worldview!" Keep a few things in mind:

- Use short movie clips if you do not have time to show an entire film.

- Show a variety of movies—comedy, action, science fiction, etc.—so students see that every film has a worldview.

- View Christian and non-Christian movies.

- Have students present their own worldview analysis of a film to the class.

If you teach another subject at a Christian school, set aside a weekly time to show a movie clip, YouTube video, popular meme, influential tweet, or other form of modern media that relates to your subject. For instance, have "Worldview Wednesday," "Film Fridays," or something similar. Make a connection between the media, your subject, and Scripture. Students will remember it and look forward to it.

critical, and keep the dialogue open. We often let our kids pick the music in the car so we can get a sense of what they want to hear and then talk about it (at times). Choose to sacrifice your music preferences so you can capitalize on the opportunity to know them and their interests.

THE OPPORTUNITY MIND-SET

Because our world is so media saturated, there are endless opportunities to help young people think biblically. But you will only find these if you *intentionally* seek them out. Deuteronomy 6:7 says to diligently teach kids when you "sit in your house, and when you walk by the way, and when you lie down, and when you rise." In other words, seize opportunities that naturally arise throughout the course of the day to remind your kids of biblical truth. Here are a few opportunities to consider:

POPULAR SONGS

Using popular music allows for a number of ways to teach Christian worldview to young people:

- Open the pop music Top 50 song list (it's available in Spotify or iTunes) and examine the list of song titles with your student(s). What do the titles *alone* tell us about the worldview embraced by our culture? How does this worldview differ from a Christian worldview?

- Listen to one of the songs on the list (if you're a parent, this opportunity may simply arise while driving in the car). What kind of worldview do the lyrics promote? Is the artist trying to influence the culture? If so, is he or she doing this subtly or more overtly? How could the lyrics be *changed* to reflect the truth of the Christian worldview?

- Do an internet search for an artist interview related to a popular song. What does the artist say that reveals his or her worldview? What insight does the artist give to help us interpret the song's lyrics?

- I (J. Warner) have played on worship teams for several years. As a youth pastor, I selected a current *pop* song and a current *Christian* (or worship) song from a similar musical genre (rock, rap, alternative, folk, etc.) and played them for my youth group with the words posted for everyone to see. I then asked the questions: How are the two songs lyrically different? How does each artist proclaim his or her worldview?

YOUTUBE VIDEOS

YouTube is the search engine of choice for Gen Zers, watching it for information *and* for entertainment. Given how much they engage with the platform, it is vital we invite them to reflect on how it may

IF YOU'RE A PARENT
HAVE A SUMMER MOVIE EXTRAVAGANZA

Recently I (Sean) came up with a plan to help my older kids engage media more thoughtfully. During summertime, we watched a number of different movies and discussed them as a family. Here are some things I did to make the time meaningful:

• I picked films that were both interesting and had themes we wanted to discuss with our kids. For instance, we watched *42*, which is the story of Jackie Robinson, and then discussed race relations.

• Watch both recent and older films. My kids thoroughly enjoyed *The Elephant Man* (1980), which is filmed in black and white. It raised great questions about human dignity, and they could see how filmmaking has evolved over time.

• If a movie bombs, don't give up. I thought my kids would enjoy *The Apostle* with Robert Duvall, but I was totally wrong. They still give me a hard time about it today, but we did have some good conversation nonetheless.

• Find a way to motivate your kids. We have some media boundaries in our home, so our kids did not expect to watch endless movies all summer. Thus, we framed the "extravaganza" as a compromise.

• Have fun. Don't worry if every discussion is not as deep as you'd like.

influence them and their peers. Here are a few simple steps we can take:

• Find a popular YouTube video. Open up YouTube and see what videos are currently trending, ask students what videos are popular, or simply be alert for when an interesting one comes to your attention.

• Show it to your students. This could be in class if you're a teacher, from the stage if you're a youth pastor, or in the car or at a meal if you're a parent.

• Ask a few questions: Why do you think this video is so popular? Why did the creator make it? What does its popularity reveal about culture today? What positive elements does it have? Any negative elements? What ideas are being promoted?

Do you agree or disagree with the ideas? What
story (worldview) is being told in the video?

ARTICLE OR BLOG FROM A SKEPTIC

One of the best ways to engage students is by reading an article or
blog from a skeptic. This may pique their interest because it comes
from a hostile perspective. Doing this shows confidence in our
Christian position and that we are not afraid of a challenge. Search
Google for a relevant article, or simply ask a skeptic you know for
an article he or she finds convincing. Then follow the simple three-
pronged approach developed by our friend Natasha Crain:[4]

- First, cut through the clutter. In other words, what
  claim is actually being made? Is it an emotional
  attack? Or is there some substance? Clear away
  secondary issues and help students have clarity
  on the actual challenge being raised.
- Second, test the claim for relevance. In other
  words, what follows if the claim is true? For
  instance, if someone claimed to have found the
  body of Jesus, then Christianity would be false
  (see 1 Corinthians 15:14, 17). The resurrection
  of Jesus is a *central* claim. But what about the
  claim that Christians are hypocrites? Would this
  undermine Christianity in the same way? No.
  It would merely show that Christians fail to live

out their beliefs. Nothing follows for the truth of Christianity from Christian hypocrisy. Before addressing the challenge, help students see what is at stake by testing it for relevance.

- Third, decide how to investigate. It is a good idea to do some research *before* bringing the skeptical challenge to your students, but the key is to help them learn how to find answers themselves. Search apologetics books. Peruse websites. Talk to your pastor. Contact an expert. Help them see the wealth of available resources to answer tough questions. (We both have articles, videos, and books on our websites that address a range of apologetics questions.)

CURRENT EVENTS

Daily news events are a wonderful opportunity to help students understand and get involved with culture. Since there is a Christian perspective on *everything*, we can engage students on a number of different kinds of stories: politics, sports, ethics, comparative religions, and more. Here are a few things we both regularly do with our own kids, in our speaking, and in the classroom:

- We share stories of Christians living out their faith. For instance, when NFL quarterback Drew Brees broke the all-time passing-yard record, he told his kids, "Nothing's given, everything's earned.

God has equipped us for great works and I tell them that every night."[5] I (Sean) shared this with my own kids and with my high school students.

- We look for the Christian worldview in the news. I (J. Warner) write regularly for national news outlets, highlighting the connection between current events and the Christian faith. If you closely pay attention, you'll start to observe the overlap between news stories and the Christian worldview. Each day, look for stories about sin, human nature, justice, ethics, or science, and you will find stories with faith connections.

- We talk about current events. My (Sean's) parents regularly engaged my sisters and me in dialogue about news stories and asked us what we thought (typically at the dinner table or in the car). While they would share their views, their main goal was to engage us in conversation about events of the day and to help us think biblically.

Many other means of helping students engage culture are available. Discuss a social media post, analyze a new research study, or talk about an interesting commercial. Regardless of the specifics, the approach is the same: be on the alert for an opportunity, experience it together, and then discuss.

Remember, the point in each of these examples is not to lecture kids about an offensive tweet or sexually explicit YouTube video

SOMETHING TIMEWORTHY

With which form of media are you most familiar?

_____

With which form of media are you least familiar?

_____

_____

_____

How might you improve your familiarity with pop culture and media to better engage the young people in your life?

_____

_____

_____

(although there may be times for that), but instead to engage young people in worldview conversations. Young people can learn to think critically about both the medium of communication _and_ the message behind it. Parents can casually do this in the car, at the dinner table, or any place you're waiting together. Youth pastors can work these examples into a sermon, or into an informal conversation with students. Christian school teachers can spare a few moments in class to make a connection between their subject and spiritual truth.

You can also teach parents, pastors, and other youth influencers how to find out what is trending on Twitter or BuzzFeed. This helps equip adults to have thoughtful conversations with young people when you are not present.

At times you may be able to have a lengthier discussion with students. Sometimes you may have just a few moments. We suggest not trying to make _everything_ spiritual and avoid forcing an unnatural discussion. On the other hand, don't underestimate the power of a good exchange with a young person and the doors it may open in the future. I (Sean) will never forget the conversation with my parents in high school over _Schindler's List_. We aim to have this kind of dialogue regularly with young people and hope you will too.

LOVE *BEGINS*

Since you stayed with us this far, there is a good chance you may be feeling *overwhelmed* right now. Even though this book is short, it is packed full of strategies for equipping the next generation to think and live biblically. You might be thinking, *Where do I even start?*

Let us close with a final suggestion: *if you love this generation, simply begin with one or two strategies, and then keep going.* Please don't feel like you must have all your "ducks in a row" before acting. Simply ask what strategy you can implement, or improve, and then go for it.

You have probably heard the aphorism attributed to Voltaire, "The best is the enemy of the good." In the case of training the next generation, this is unmistakably true. Don't feel you have to do *everything* to make a difference. We have been training students for decades and are still learning new strategies in parenting, speaking, mentoring, and writing. The key is to begin by doing *something*.

Writing a book is a massive task. It's intimidating and time consuming. Even though we have written or edited many books, it is always a challenge to begin a new one. In fact, when the time came to write *this* book, I (Sean) found myself coming up with mental excuses to put it off. It seemed daunting amid everything else I had to do as a professor, teacher, speaker, parent, and blogger!

Yet one of the best pieces of advice we have ever heard about writing is simply to begin. Seriously, *just begin*. At some point, you have to sit down and start outlining or writing. Taking this first step, as difficult as it can be, starts the process that ultimately translates into a book.

The same is true for impacting this next generation. There are many steps to take, as we've describe in these pages. The key is simply to begin the process with a *first* step. And then take a *second* step. And so on. Over time, you can make a difference in the lives of young people. When I (J. Warner) first began my seminary degree, I knew it would take me six or seven years to finish. I also knew those years would pass—*whether I achieved the degree or not*. Given that reality, I concluded I would rather be seven years older *with* a degree than *without* one.

If you're raising, teaching, or pastoring young people, the years are going to pass whether you adopt the strategies in this book or not. You might as well start; the first step you take is up to you. We suggest beginning with something that feels manageable. Start with a strategy you are confident could work in your unique situation. Write it down. Share it with someone. Implement it. As you have some success, try something harder. Then keep going!

While you will certainly feel some "bumps and bruises" along the way, you can make a lasting difference. If you feel inadequate to train this generation, please know that God has equipped you to make an eternal difference with Gen Z. That's right—God has equipped *you*.

Don't compare yourself to anyone else. Your job (and our job) is simply to be *faithful*. Just be the person God has made you to be. Trust that God is the One who ultimately transforms lives. And remember, God will supply us with *all our needs* (Philippians 4:19).

Time is short. This generation faces more intellectual, moral, and emotional challenges—just one click away—than any previous generation. And yet they have unbelievable promise. Now is the time to begin. Forget about yesterday. Don't worry about tomorrow. Today is the day to begin *so that the next generation will know*.

APPENDIX

CURRICULUMS

Small Group Curriculums

Evidence for Faith 8-part Apologetics Course by Josh McDowell and Sean McDowell (Download Youth Ministry: www.dymuniversity.com/store/5jW9SR5Y)

Journey: Advocates by Sean McDowell and Awana (Awana: www.awanaym.org/journey/advocates)

Cold-Case Christianity 8-week Video Curriculum by J. Warner Wallace (David C Cook)

God's Crime Scene 8-week Video Curriculum by J. Warner Wallace (David C Cook)

Forensic Faith 8-week Video Curriculum by J. Warner Wallace (David C Cook)

TrueU by Focus on the Family (Focus on the Family)

Big Questions: Developing a Christ-Centered Apologetic by Andy McLean, William Lane Craig, J. P. Moreland, Sean McDowell, and Craig Hazen (LifeWay)

Christian School Curriculums

Understanding the Times High School Curriculum by Jeff Myers (David C Cook)

I Don't Have Enough Faith to Be an Atheist Curriculum by Frank Turek and Chuck Winter (Apologia Educational Ministries)

Deep Roots Bible Curriculum (Defendable Faith Institute, available at www.deeprootsbible.com)

Websites

Case Makers Academy (for kids ages 8–12): www.casemakersacademy.com

Five Things Every Teenager Needs to Build a Lasting Faith by Jonathan Morrow: http://5thingseveryteenagerneeds.com

CONFERENCES

Summit Student Conferences (www.summit.org): A life-changing twelve-day worldview training experience for students in Colorado, Tennessee, and Pennsylvania.

reTHINK Apologetics Student Conferences (www.rethinkapologetics.com): Weekend apologetics conferences featuring leading apologists and thinkers today tailored uniquely for students.

Impact 360 Immersion (www.impact360institute.org): Two-week summer worldview and apologetics experience for high school students in Pine Mountain, Georgia.

Wheatstone Academy (www.christianadulthood.org): One-week worldview experience designed to help students ask deep, meaningful questions, think Christianly about the arts and culture, and cultivate their own faith.

Maven Truth Conferences (www.maventruth.com): Weekend apologetics conferences featuring leading apologists and thinkers today tailored—much like the reTHINK conferences—uniquely for students.

THEOLOGY RESOURCES

Bible

The Apologetics Study Bible for Students, contributions by Sean McDowell and J. Warner Wallace (Holman Bible Publishers: CSBible.com)

Books

Christian Theology by Millard J. Erickson (Baker Academic)

Systematic Theology: An Introduction to Biblical Doctrine by Wayne Grudem (Zondervan)

Systematic Theology: In One Volume by Norm Geisler (Bethany House Publishers)

Websites

Theopedia: www.theopedia.com

Bible Gateway: www.biblegateway.com

APOLOGETICS RESOURCES

Books

Cold-Case Christianity: A Homicide Detective Investigates the Claims of the Gospels by J. Warner Wallace (David C Cook) – Kids edition for ages 8–12 also available

God's Crime Scene: A Cold-Case Detective Examines the Evidence for a Divinely Created Universe by J. Warner Wallace (David C Cook) – Kids edition for ages 8-12 also available

Forensic Faith: A Homicide Detective Makes the Case for a More Reasonable, Evidential Christian Faith by J. Warner Wallace (David C Cook) – Kids edition for ages 8-12 also available

Is God Just a Human Invention? by Sean McDowell and Jonathan Morrow (Kregel Publications)

Ethix: Being Bold in a Whatever World by Sean McDowell (B&H Publishing)

Understanding Intelligent Design: Everything You Need to Know in Plain Language by William A. Dembski and Sean McDowell (Harvest House Publishers)

More Than a Carpenter by Josh D. McDowell and Sean McDowell (Tyndale)

Evidence That Demands a Verdict: Life-Changing Truth for a Skeptical World by Josh McDowell and Sean McDowell (Thomas Nelson)

I Don't Have Enough Faith to Be an Atheist by Norman L. Geisler and Frank Turek (Crossway Books)

Welcome to College: A Christ-Follower's Guide for the Journey by Jonathan Morrow (Kregel Publications)

The Case for Christ: A Journalist's Personal Investigation of the Evidence for Jesus by Lee Strobel (Zondervan) – Student edition for ages 11–13 also available

The Case for Faith: A Journalist Investigates the Toughest Objections to Christianity by Lee Strobel (Zondervan) – Student edition for ages 11–13 also available

The Case for a Creator: A Journalist Investigates Scientific Evidence That Points toward God by Lee Strobel (Zondervan) – Student edition for ages 11–13 also available

Love Thy Body: Answering Hard Questions about Life and Sexuality by Nancy R. Pearcey (Baker Books)

A Practical Guide to Culture: Helping the Next Generation Navigate Today's World by John Stonestreet and Brett Kunkle (David C Cook)

Websites

Sean McDowell: https://seanmcdowell.org

Cold-Case Christianity (J. Warner Wallace): http://coldcasechristianity.com

BreakPoint: http://breakpoint.org

Videos

Sean McDowell YouTube Channel (at www.youtube.com)

Cold-Case Christianity YouTube Channel (at www.youtube.com)

Reasonable Faith animated videos
(available at www.reasonablefaith.org)
Impact 360 videos
(available at www.impact360institute.org)

TAB TRIP RESOURCES

Brett Kunkle, www.maventruth.com. Brett leads a team that takes students on "immersive experiences" like the Utah and Berkeley mission trips.

EXAMPLE OF SPIRITUAL SURVEY

This survey was first developed by Brett Kunkle from Maven (www.maventruth.com). The goal of this survey is simply to generate meaningful spiritual conversations:

Do you believe in a supreme being or higher power?
Why or why not?
What do you think he, she, or it is like, and why?
Do you believe truth exists? If so, do you think we can know truth?
Is there such a thing as objective/absolute truth?
Is there religious truth? If so, how do we find it?
Do you believe there are moral facts (right and wrong) that everyone should follow? Or do you believe that morality is relative to individuals or cultures?
Why or why not?
Do you believe in an afterlife?

Why or why not?

If yes, what do you think the afterlife is like?

Who do you believe Jesus was?

Why do you believe this about Jesus?

Where do you get most of your information about Jesus?

What do you think about Christianity?

Why do you believe this?

What has given you this impression?

SAMPLE THEOLOGICAL TAB TRIP ITINERARY (UTAH)

Day One

Meet early in the morning, pack vehicles, drive to Salt Lake City

Arrive in Salt Lake City in time for dinner

Drive to host church, meet their leadership team and unpack

Free time, debrief, review the next day's schedule, pray, and go to bed

Day Two

Wake up, eat breakfast

Morning worship, devotional, study and solitude time

Mormon training with a local Christian apologist

Pack sack lunches and dinners

Travel to Temple Square to tour the Church Museum, Beehive House, and Visitor Center

Travel to Donut Falls to hike, eat dinner, debrief, and worship

Return to host church and go to bed

Day Three

Wake up, eat breakfast

Morning worship, devotional, study and solitude time

Pack sack lunches

Return to Temple Square to engage people in spiritual conversations and evangelize

Eat lunch in the grassy area by our cars, then return to Temple Square

Eat dinner at a local restaurant

Return to host church for Mormon training with a local Christian apologist

Debrief and share stories about the day, review tomorrow's schedule, free time, then go to bed

Day Four

Wake up, eat breakfast

Morning worship, devotional, study and solitude time

Pack sack lunches, then drive to local Christian apologist for training

Return to Temple Square to engage people in spiritual conversations and evangelize

Return to host church for dinner

Debrief and share stories about the day, review tomorrow's schedule, free time, then go to bed

Day Five

Wake up, eat breakfast

Morning worship, devotional, study and solitude time

Travel to Brigham Young University for lunch in the cafeteria and spiritual conversations with BYU students

Participate in door-to-door witnessing in the neighborhood around BYU

Travel to Sundance resort, eat dinner, explore the resort, and have free time

Return to host church, debrief, review tomorrow's schedule, and go to bed

Day Six

Wake up, eat breakfast, pack sack lunches

Pack all items into cars for departure from host church

Clean the host church, leave for Manti

Eat lunch in a local park in Manti, participate in training session with local Christian apologist

Settle in with host residence in Manti, unpack the cars, then free time and dinner

Travel to Manti Temple and participate in Miracle Pageant outreach/street witnessing

Watch the Miracle Pageant, then return to host residence and go to bed

Day Seven

Wake up, eat breakfast

Morning worship, devotional, debrief the prior night's activity

Mormon training with a local Christian apologist

Eat lunch, then free time at a local lake

Return to host house, study time

Travel to Manti Temple and participate in Miracle Pageant outreach/street witnessing

Go out to dinner with other local Christian believers

Return to host house, debrief, go to bed

Day Eight

Wake up early, pack up, load luggage into vehicles

Eat breakfast, clean the host residence, and depart for home

Arrive home after stopping for two meals

SAMPLE APOLOGETICS TAB TRIP ITINERARY (BERKELEY)

Day One

Meet early in the morning, pack vehicles, drive to Berkeley

Arrive in Berkeley at host church, meet their leadership team, and unpack

Travel to Berkeley and eat dinner at a restaurant

Tour the UC Berkeley campus and pray over it

Return to host church and conduct "role-playing" scenarios

Train with a local Christian apologist

Assign topics students will present (and record) on the last day, then go to bed

Day Two

Wake up, eat breakfast

Morning worship, devotional, study and solitude time

Atheist presentation by local atheist speaker followed by student Q and A

Debrief atheist presentation

Travel to Berkeley, eat on Telegraph Avenue

Conduct spiritual surveys at Sproul Plaza on the campus of Berkeley

Return to host church, study time for student presentations, then eat dinner

Watch a video debate from William Lane Craig, then discuss and debrief

Free time, work on presentations, then go to bed

Day Three

Wake up, eat breakfast

Morning worship, devotional, study and solitude time

Attend local presentation from Unitarian Universalist pastor, then attend their church service

Eat lunch at a restaurant

Drive to Pier 39, Fisherman's Wharf, Golden Gate Bridge, or Alcatraz

Conduct spiritual surveys after eating and shopping

Return to host church, free time, work on presentations, then go to bed

Day Four

Wake up, eat breakfast

Morning worship, devotional, study and solitude time

Atheist presentation by local atheist speaker followed by student Q and A

Debrief atheist presentation, eat lunch

Atheist presentation by local atheist speaker followed by student Q and A

Debrief atheist presentation, free time to work on presentations, then eat dinner

Travel to Berkeley to engage student atheist group in table discussions

Return to host church, debrief, free time, work on presentations, then go to bed

Day Five

Wake up, eat breakfast

Atheist presentation by local atheist speaker followed by student Q and A

Debrief atheist presentation, eat lunch

Travel to Berkeley, conduct spiritual surveys at Sproul Plaza on Berkeley campus

Eat dinner, return to host church, then watch student presentations on assigned topics

Debrief, worship, then go to bed

Day Six

Wake up, eat breakfast

Pack the cars, clean the host church, depart for home

Stop and eat lunch on the way home

Arrive at home in time for dinner

ACKNOWLEDGMENTS

A book like this is not possible without a supportive team. We would like to thank Jonathan Morrow, Susie Wallace, and Jonathan McKee for offering suggestions and edits on early drafts of this book. We also appreciate the massive research efforts of Joel Hughes and Kendall Brewer in tracking down stories, statistics, and studies on Generation Z, and the thoughtful contributions of Timothy Fox in helping us develop the participant's guide.

We are also grateful for our continuing partnership with the David C Cook publishing team and for the contributions of Stephanie Bennett, Jack Campbell, Nick Lee, and Wendi Lord. Thanks for your guidance, input, and patience.

Lastly, thanks to our agent and friend, Mark Sweeney, for his wisdom and encouragement.

NOTES

CHAPTER 1: LOVE *RESPONDS*

1. "Social Media, Social Life: Teens Reveal Their Experiences (2018)," Common Sense Media, accessed January 20, 2019, www.commonsensemedia.org /research/social-media-social-life-2018.

2. For a complete list of the surveys related to the departure of young people from the church, please read: J. Warner Wallace, "UPDATED: Are Young People Really Leaving Christianity?," http://coldcasechristianity.com/2018/are -young-people-really-leaving-christianity/.

3. Lee Miller and Wei Lu, "Gen Z Is Set to Outnumber Millennials within a Year," *Chicago Tribune*, August 20, 2018, www.chicagotribune.com/news/nation-world/ct-gen-z-millennials-20180820-story.html.

4. "The Nielsen Total Audience Report: Q1 2017," July 12, 2017, www.nielsen.com/us /en/insights/reports/2017/the-nielsen-total-audience-report-q1-2017.html.

5. "Atheism Doubles among Generation Z," Barna Group, January 24, 2018, www.barna.com/research/atheism-doubles-among-generation-z/.

6. "Spirituality in Higher Education: Students' Search for Meaning and Purpose," Higher Education Research Institute, University of California, Los Angeles, accessed July 31, 2018, www.spirituality.ucla.edu/.

7. J. Warner Wallace, "UPDATED: Are Young People Really Leaving Christianity?," Cold-Case Christianity, January 12, 2019, http://coldcasechristianity. com/2018/are-young-people-really-leaving-christianity/.

8. "What Is Sticky Faith?," Fuller Youth Institute, accessed January 21, 2019, https://fulleryouthinstitute.org/stickyfaith.

9. Christian Smith, *Soul Searching: The Religious and Spiritual Lives of American Teenagers* (New York: Oxford University Press, 2005), 89.

10. Michael Lipka, "Why America's 'Nones' Left Religion Behind," Pew Research Center, August 24, 2016, www.pewresearch.org/fact-tank/2016/08/24/why-americas-nones-left-religion-behind/ (wording changed slightly to fit the context of this chapter). See also "Choosing a New Church or House of Worship," Pew Research Center, August 23, 2016, www.pewforum.org/2016/08/23/choosing-a-new-church-or-house-of-worship/.

11. Mark M. Gray, "Young People Are Leaving the Faith. Here's Why," *OSV Newsweekly*, August 27, 2016, www.osv.com/OSVNewsweekly/PapalVisit/Articles/Article/TabId/2727/ArtMID/20933/ArticleID/20512/Young-people-are-leaving-the-faith-Heres-why.aspx.

12. I (Sean) have personally heard reasons like these before. For similar responses and information, see *Gen Z: The Culture, Beliefs, and Motivations Shaping the Next Generation* (Ventura, CA: Barna Group, 2018).

13. Daniel Cox, "College Professors Aren't Killing Religion," FiveThirtyEight, October 10, 2017, https://fivethirtyeight.com/features/college-professors-arent-killing-religion/.

14. Larry Alex Taunton, "Listening to Young Atheists: Lessons for a Stronger Christianity," *Atlantic*, June 6, 2013, www.theatlantic.com/national/archive/2013/06/listening-to-young-atheists-lessons-for-a-stronger-christianity/276584/; and Gray, "Young People Are Leaving the Faith," www.osv.com/OSVNewsweekly/PapalVisit/Articles/Article/TabId/2727/ArtMID/20933/ArticleID/20512/Young-people-are-leaving-the-faith-Heres-why.aspx.

15. "When Americans Say They Believe in God, What Do They Mean?," Pew Research Center, April 25, 2018, www.pewforum.org/2018/04/25/when-americans-say-they-believe-in-god-what-do-they-mean/.

16. Vern L. Bengtson, *Families and Faith: How Religion Is Passed Down across Generations* (New York: Oxford University Press, 2013), 19; see also chapter 5, "The Unexpected Importance of Grandparents (and Great-Grandparents)."

17. "When Americans Become Christians," National Association of Evangelicals, Spring 2015, www.nae.net/when-americans-become-christians/.

CHAPTER 2: LOVE *UNDERSTANDS*

1. Thanks to our friend Jeff Myers, in his presentation for the Cultivate Project, for drawing our attention to these kinds of generational comparisons.

2. J. Walter Thompson Intelligence Edudemic Survey (2012), as cited by Sparks and Honey Consulting and Advisory, "Meet Generation Z," SlideShare, June 17, 2014, www.slideshare.net/sparksandhoney/generation-z-final-june-17/28-They_multitask_across_5_screens28Age.

3. "Social Media, Social Life: Teens Reveal Their Experiences (2018)," Common Sense Media, accessed January 20, 2019, www.commonsensemedia.org /research/social-media-social-life-2018.

4. "Generation Z Facts and Stats Marketers Need to Know [Infographic]," Acorn, accessed March 15, 2018, www.acorninfluence.com/blog/generation -z-stats-facts-marketers-infographic/.

5. Lenna Garibian, "Gen-Z Trusts Mobile, Social Content More Than Other Generations Do," MarketingProfs, April 4, 2013, www.marketingprofs.com /charts/2013/10462/gen-z-trusts-mobile-social-content-more-than -other-generations.

6. "Attention Span Statistics," Statistic Brain Institute, March 2, 2018, www.statisticbrain.com/attention-span-statistics/.

7. Alex Williams, "Move Over, Millennials, Here Comes Generation Z," *New York Times*, September 18, 2015.

8. *Gen Z: The Culture, Beliefs, and Motivations Shaping the Next Generation* (Ventura, CA: Barna Group, 2018), 46.

9. *Gen Z*, 46.

10. "Generation Z: Marketing's Next Big Audience," Marketo, in Sparks and Honey Consulting and Advisory, "Meet Generation Z," SlideShare, June 17, 2014, www.slideshare.net/sparksandhoney/generation-z-final-june-17/28-They _multitask_across_5_screens28Age.

11. Innovation Group, "Meet Generation Z," report, J. Walter Thompson Intelligence, May 18, 2015, www.jwtintelligence.com/2015/05/meet -generation-z/.

12. Ryan Scott, "Get Ready for Generation Z," *Forbes*, November 28, 2016, www.forbes.com/sites/causeintegration/2016/11/28/get-ready-for -generation-z/#7251db6c2204.

13. Susanna Schrobsdorff, "The Kids Are Not All Right," *Time*, November 7, 2016, 47.

14. Erin Anderssen, "Through the Eyes of Generation Z," *Globe and Mail*, November 12, 2017, www.theglobeandmail.com/news/national/through -the-eyes-of-generation-z/article30571914/.

15. Jean Twenge, *iGen: Why Today's Super-Connected Kids Are Growing Up Less Rebellious, More Tolerant, Less Happy—and Completely Unprepared for Adulthood* (New York: Atria, 2017), 93.

16. Joel Stein, "Millennials: The Me Me Me Generation," *Time*, May 20, 2013, http://time.com/247/millennials-the-me-me-me-generation/.

17. "Getting to Know Gen Z: How the Pivotal Generation Is Different from Millennials," Barkley and FutureCast, January 2017, www.barkleyus.com/wp -content/uploads/2017/01/FutureCast_The-Pivotal-Generation.pdf.

18. Twenge, *iGen*, 132.

19. Jonathan Morrow, "Only 4 Percent of Gen Z Have a Biblical Worldview: New 2018 Barna and Impact 360 Institute Research Shows," Impact 360 Institute, accessed January 21, 2019, www.impact360institute.org/articles /4-percent-gen-z-biblical-worldview/.

20. "Innovation Imperative: Portrait of Generation Z," Northeastern University and FTI Consulting, November 18, 2014, www.fticonsulting.com/~/media/Files/us -files/insights/reports/generationz.pdf.

CHAPTER 3: LOVE *RELATES*

1. Ellie Polack, "New Cigna Study Reveals Loneliness at Epidemic Levels in America," Cigna, May 1, 2018, www.cigna.com/newsroom/news-releases /2018/new-cigna-study-reveals-loneliness-at-epidemic-levels-in-america.

2. Paul Vitz, "The Psychology of Atheism," chapter 7 in *A Place for Truth: Leading Thinkers Explore Life's Hardest Questions*, ed. Dallas Willard (Downers Grove, IL: InterVarsity, 2010), 136–53.

3. Joan Hope, "Get Your Campus Ready for Generation Z," *The Successful Registrar* 16, no. 7 (September 2016): 6.

4. Sean Keach, "Watching Over You: Teens Want Parents to Restrict What They Do Online, Study Suggests," *Sun*, February 6, 2018, www.thesun.co.uk/tech /5506367/teens-parents-parental-controls-online-restrictions/.

5. Jingjing Jiang, "How Teens and Parents Navigate Screen Time and Device Distractions," Pew Research, August 22, 2018, www.pewinternet.org/2018/08 /22/how-teens-and-parents-navigate-screen-time-and-device-distractions/.

6. Mark Abadi, "Adults Who Went Undercover at a High School Found Seven Things People Don't Realize about Life for Teenagers Today," Business Insider, February 12, 2018, www.businessinsider.com/undercover -high-teenagers-lives-2018-2.

CHAPTER 4: LOVE *EQUIPS*

1. *Gen Z: The Culture, Beliefs, and Motivations Shaping the Next Generation* (Ventura, CA: Barna Group, 2018).

2. David Kinnaman and Gabe Lyons, *UnChristian: What a New Generation Really Thinks about Christianity ... and Why It Matters* (Grand Rapids, MI: Baker Books, 2007), 81.

3. Find out more about Summit ministries at www.summit.org.

4. *Gen Z*, 25.

5. Julie Beck, "The New Age of Astrology: In a Stressful, Data-Driven Era, Many Young People Find Comfort and Insight in the Zodiac—Even If They Don't Exactly Believe in It," *Atlantic*, January 16, 2018, www.theatlantic.com/health /archive/2018/01/the-new-age-of-astrology/550034/.

6. John C. Maxwell, *Intentional Living: Choosing a Life That Matters* (Nashville: Hachette, 2015), ebook section "Intentional Living Encourages Us to Finish Well."

7. *Abraham Kuyper: A Centennial Reader*, ed. James D. Bratt (Grand Rapids, MI: William B. Eerdmans, 1998), 461.

8. James K. A. Smith, *You Are What You Love: The Spiritual Power of Habit* (Grand Rapids, MI: Brazos, 2016).

9. "Jonathan Morrow on Building Lasting Faith in Gen Z," Barna, July 19, 2018, www.barna.com/gen-z-qa-with-jonathan-morrow/.

CHAPTER 5: LOVE *IGNITES*

1. "Atheism Doubles among Generation Z," Barna Group, January 24, 2018, www.barna.com/research/atheism-doubles-among-generation-z/.

2. Dictionary.com, s.v. "apathy," accessed January 23, 2019, www.dictionary.com /browse/apathy.

3. K. Robert Beshears, "Apatheism: Engaging the Western Pantheon of Spiritual Indifference," Southern Baptist Theological Seminary, April 2016, https://hcommons.org/deposits/objects/hc:11094/datastreams /CONTENT/content.

4. Paul Rowan Brian and Ben Sixsmith, "Apatheism Is More Damaging to Christianity Than Atheism and Antitheism," *Public Discourse*, August 13, 2018, www.thepublicdiscourse.com/2018/08/21919/.

5. "Silent and Solo: How Americans Pray," Barna Group, August 15, 2017, www.barna.com/research/silent-solo-americans-pray/.

6. "Porn in the Digital Age: New Research Reveals 10 Trends," Barna Group, April 6, 2-16, www.barna.com/research/porn-in-the-digital-age-new-research -reveals-10-trends/.

7. "Pornography Survey Statistics," Proven Men, survey conducted by Barna Group, 2014, www.provenmen.org/pornography-survey-statistics-2014/.

8. Theodore Roosevelt, "American Ideals in Education," speech to Iowa State Teacher's Association, November 4, 1910, reel 421, Theodore Roosevelt papers, Manuscript Division, Library of Congress, Washington DC.

CHAPTER 6: LOVE *TRAINS*

1. "Dig Deeper: Critical Thinking in the Digital Age," MindEdge, accessed January 23, 2019, https://mindedge.com/page/dig-deeper.

2. For more information about the TRAIN acronym, please refer to J. Warner Wallace, *Forensic Faith: A Homicide Detective Makes the Case for a More Reasonable, Evidential Christian Faith* (Colorado Springs: David C Cook, 2017), esp. ch. 2, "Targeted Training."

3. Bob Smietana, "LifeWay Research: Americans Are Fond of the Bible, Don't Actually Read It," LifeWay, April 25, 2017, https://lifewayresearch. com/2017/04/25/lifeway-research-americans-are-fond-of-the-bible -dont-actually-read-it/.

4. Russ Rankin, "Study: Bible Engagement in Churchgoers' Hearts, Not Always Practiced," LifeWay, January 1, 2014, www.lifeway.com/en/articles/research -survey-bible-engagement-churchgoers.

5. "Competing Worldviews Influence Today's Christians," Barna Group, May 9, 2017, www.barna.com/research/competing-worldviews-influence-todays -christians/, italics added.

6. John Stonestreet, "The High Price of Utilitarian Thinking: Bad Ideas Have Victims," CNS News, April 19, 2017, www.cnsnews.com/commentary/john -stonestreet/high-price-utilitarian-thinking-bad-ideas-have-victims.

7. For more about Dr. Parrott, see his Northwest University faculty page at www. northwestu.edu/social-behavioral/faculty/les-parrott/ (accessed January 23, 2019), and read about his identity categories here: Amy Bellows, "Your Teen's Search for Identity," Psych Central, October 8, 2018, https://psychcentral.com/lib/your-teens-search-for-identity/.

8. Arlener D. Turner, Christine E. Smith, and Jason C. Ong, "Is Purpose in Life Associated with Less Sleep Disturbance in Older Adults?," *Sleep Science and Practice* 1 (July 10, 2017): 14, https://sleep.biomedcentral.com/articles /10.1186/s41606-017-0015-6.

9. Nathan A. Lewis, et al., "Purpose in Life and Cognitive Functioning in Adulthood," *Aging, Neuropsychology, and Cognition* 24 (November 7, 2016): 662–71, www.tandfonline.com/doi/full/10.1080/13825585.2016.1251549.

10. Patrick L. Hill, et al., "Purpose in Life in Emerging Adulthood: Development and Validation of a New Brief Measure," *Journal of Positive Psychology* 11 (June 3, 2015): 237–45, www.tandfonline.com/doi/full/10.1080/17439760.2015.1048817.

11. Barbara L. Fredrickson, et al., "A Functional Genomic Perspective on Human Well-Being," *Proceedings of the National Academy of Sciences of the United States of America*, August 13, 2013, www.pnas.org/content/110/33/13684.

12. Andrew Steptoe, Angus Deaton, Arthur A. Stone, "Subjective Wellbeing, Health, and Ageing," *Lancet* 385 (February 14, 2015): 640–48, www.thelancet.com/journals/lancet/article/PIIS0140-6736(13)61489-0/fulltext.

13. Stephen Cranney, "Do People Who Believe in God Report More Meaning in Their Lives?: The Existential Effects of Belief," *Journal for the Scientific Study of Religion* 52 (September 2013): 638–46, https://onlinelibrary.wiley.com/doi/abs/10.1111/jssr.12046.

CHAPTER 7: LOVE *EXPLORES*

1. To learn more about Brett Kunkle and his powerful ministry to young people (and to schedule your own worldview mission trip), please visit www.maventruth.com.

2. Corey Seemiller and Meghan Grace, *Generation Z Goes to College* (San Francisco: Jossey-Bass, 2016), as referenced by La Monica Everett-Haynes, "Generation Z: A New Class of Students Arrives," University of Arizona, January 28, 2016, https://uanews.arizona.edu/story/generation-z-new-class-students-arrives.

3. For more on this, please see J. Warner Wallace, *Forensic Faith: A Homicide Detective Makes the Case for a More Reasonable, Evidential Christian Faith* (Colorado Springs: David C Cook, 2017).

4. For more information on Utah Lighthouse Ministry, please visit www.utlm.org.

5. For more information on Mormon Research Ministry, please visit www.mrm.org.

CHAPTER 8: LOVE *ENGAGES*

1. See Jean Twenge, *iGen: Why Today's Super-Connected Kids Are Growing Up Less Rebellious, More Tolerant, Less Happy—and Completely Unprepared*

for Adulthood (New York: Atria, 2017), esp. ch. 4, "Insecure: The New Mental Health Crisis."

2. Donna Freitas, *The Happiness Effect: How Social Media Is Driving a Generation to Appear Perfect at Any Cost* (New York: Oxford University Press, 2017).

3. As we saw in chapter 3, 69 percent of teens think parental controls online are a good idea. Sean Keach, "Watching Over You: Teens Want Parents to Restrict What They Do Online, Study Suggests," *Sun*, February 6, 2018, www.thesun .co.uk/tech/5506367/teens-parents-parental-controls-online-restrictions/.

4. This is from her presentation "Three Critical Thinking Skills Every Child Should Have," which she sent to us personally. See natashacrain.com for information about her ministry.

5. Nancy Flory, "Saints' QB Breaks Yardage Record, Tells His Kids 'God Has Equipped Us for Great Works,'" *Stream*, October 9, 2018, https://stream.org/saints-qb -breaks-yardage-record-tells-kids-god-equipped-us-great-works/.